THE AUTHENTIC LEADER AS SERVANT (ALS)

ALS I COURSE 9
SERVANTHOOD LEADERSHIP
Attributes, Principles, and Practices

SYLVANUS N. WOSU, Ph.D

THE AUTHENTIC LEADER AS SERVANT
ALS I COURSE 9
Developing Servanthood Leadership Attributes, Principles, and Practices

© Copyright 2024 by Sylvanus N. Wosu Ph.D.

Printed in the United States of America
ISBN: 979-8-9858816-9-1

All rights reserved. No part of this book may be reproduced or transmitted in any form or by any means, electronic or mechanical, including photocopying, recording, or by any information storage and retrieval system, without permission in writing from the copyright owner.

Bible quotations are from the New King James (NKJV) version of the Bible unless otherwise indicated.

Other versions used in this book are the New International Version (NIV), New Living Translation (NLT), King James Version (KJV), English Standard Version (ESV), and Good News Translation (GNT). Unless otherwise specified, NKJV should be assumed.

The views expressed in this work are solely those of the author and do not necessarily reflect the views of the publisher, and the publisher disclaims any responsibility for them.

To order additional copies of this book, contact:
Proisle Publishing Services LLC
39-67 58th Street, 1st floor
Woodside, NY 11377, USA
Phone: (+1 646-480-0129)
info@proislepublishing.com

PROISLE PUBLISHING

TABLE OF CONTENTS

FOREWORD — XI
ACKNOWLEDGMENTS — XV
DEDICATION — XIX
PREFACE — 21
    About Leader As Servant Leadership (LSL) Model — 24
    About the Authentic Leader as Servant (ALS) — 27
    About the ALS Courses — 28

CHAPTER 1
UNDERSTANDING LEADERSHIP ATTRIBUTES — 37
    Functional Definitions — 37
    Comparisons With Other Works — 42
    Principle of Leadership Attribute — 44
    Authentic Leadership Attributes — 45
    Summary 1 Understanding Leadership Process — 51

CHAPTER 2
CHARACTERISTICS OF SERVANTHOOD LEADERSHIP ATTRIBUTE — 55
    Characteristics of Servanthood Attribute — 55
    Principle of leadership Servanthood Attribute — 56
    Summary 2 Servanthood Leadership Attribute — 58

CHAPTER 3
DEVELOPING THE SERVANT'S HEART IN SERVANTHOOD — 61
    Summary 3 Developing the Servant's Heart in Servanthood Attribute — 67

CHAPTER 4
DEVELOPING A SERVANT'S HEART OF HUMILITY — 71
    A Case of the Power of Full Faith in Weakness — 88
    Summary 4 Developing Servant's Heart of Humility — 90

CHAPTER 5
DEVELOPING THE ACTS OF SERVANT-WILLINGNESS — 95
    Summary 5 Developing the Acts of Servant-Willingness — 102

CHAPTER 6
DEVELOPING THE ACTS OF SERVANTHOOD-SACRIFICE 105
The Seven Levels of Ultimate Sacrifices --------------------------------------- 107
Developing the Acts of Sacrifice-Selflessness ---------------------------------- 109
Developing the Acts of Commitment in Sacrifice ---------------------------- 112
Summary 6 Developing The Acts of Sacrifice in Servanthood -------------- 113

CHAPTER 7
DEVELOPING THE ACTS OF INTENTIONALITY 117
Summary 7 Developing the Acts of Intentionality ---------------------------- 122

CHAPTER 8
DEVELOPING THE ACTS OF SERVANTHOOD-SERVICE 125
Summery 8 Developing the Acts of Servanthood-Service ------------------- 132

TOPIC INDEX 137
REFERENCES 141

Foreword

The modern world today is obsessed with standardization and modalities. As a result, in the realm of leadership, many books have spout associated leadership theories and models and explain them as the path to follow. However, the critical dimensions that distinguish the effectiveness of any leadership process are the values and attribute the leader brings to the table; desired change is influenced by leadership styles or standards. These many standards and theories of leadership often are not in step with the changing times or the followers' needs. The trend is a bit like stocking different kinds of foods in a grocery store and expecting that they will meet everybody's needs the same way and at all times. Aisles are packed with varieties of food with expiration dates in the future, but getting the best deal on the products is what really matters to those who buy and use the products

In many ways, this is the state of leadership in the modern world. Increasingly, even leaders of public institutions are tasked with turning a profit for themselves or the organization they serve. The idea of a "leader" seems to float uneasily alongside the ranks of fundraisers or profit raisers in contrast to any kind of role model for followers or employees. That which is knowable, measurable, and marketable has surpassed the difficult intangibility of strong moral leadership attributes as the central guideline for achievement and success.

In this complicated space, Dr. Sylvanus Wosu introduces his complex idea of the Leader as a Servant Leadership, which is in this book, modeled on Christian tradition. Like all intricate ideas, Dr. Wosu's central point depends on a paradox: a person is best qualified to lead when he or she is most ready to serve. This paradox has been monopolized rhetorically by "public servants" who often serve either self-interest or the interests of specific lobbies. The Authentic Leader as Servant penetrates past the superficial concept of "serving" and details the internal state of true servitude or Servanthood.

While the book is primarily focused on the Christian model of leadership attributes such as discipleship, empathy, affection, and Servanthood, it does so not merely on the grounds of blind faith, but rather via numerous contemporary sociological and business-driven studies on how leaders should seek a leader-follower relationship that is simultaneously productive and nurturing. Dr. Wosu's most piercing insights always involve this secular–Christian dialogue. This book demonstrates that Christ's model for leadership is one that may exist successfully outside the confines of a faith relationship; it places the values of Christ's religious significance in leadership at the center of the framework. It is clear from Dr. Wosu's generous own life story of faith—a faith tested by humbling difficulties—is at the center of both his orientation and motivation for writing.

In language that is so concise, it is often illustrated in mathematical formulas; Dr. Wosu explains the deep structural integrity of Christ's Leader as the Servant Leadership model. One could imagine leaders of any doctrine benefiting from the analyses contained in these pages. The book's message repeatedly encourages the reader to imagine a scenario or reflect on memories and personal experiences to prove or test its many points. Thus, the book depends on a form of praxis, a lesson that could be or has been enacted, by the participating reader. I am very impressed at the volume and level of thinking of the author. Parts of the book involve his personal story, which is especially riveting. I cannot imagine what he had to endure, which he referred to as a" wilderness walk," to accomplish the goal he set for himself. His life stories on these pages are inspiring and stimulating.

In this way, the text eschews dogmatism in favor of the self-discovery Socratic Method of teaching and learning. The reader is not badgered into complying with a religious objective but is rather asked to consider the applicability of difficult biblical concepts in relation to modern life. It is a fascinating and very thought-provoking read.

Hence, the book does not seek to make the leader a servant, a cookie-cutter corporate buzzword, but rather asks the reader to imagine him or herself interacting with a range of concepts. One of Dr. Wosu's great strengths is his reservation when it comes to forcing his reading's interpretation on the material he presents.

The book parallels Biblical and modern leadership scenarios in ways that consistently provoke thought, and while it is clear Dr. Wosu has his particular leadership style; the space for the reader's own thoughts is always left open.

The book could not have been written in any other way with integrity. Its format and formulas are offered to the reader of the leader as a servant role that it analyzes in its pages. To find a text that instructs from this humble position is profoundly refreshing in a genre that is often packaged inside a cover with a sizeable picture of the "modest" author, smiling egotistically beneath a name spelled out in large, gold lettering. Throughout its pages, this text feels as if it serves the reader.

In the end, this is the most satisfying aspect of the book. There is no standardized approach to achieving successful leadership. There is no promise of power and a bigger payday; in fact, the book often proffers just the opposite. The reader is not encouraged to devalue the experience of leadership by finding some economic metric for marking success but is rather asked to think deeply about the most basic elements of internal and social interaction within the framework of a Christian tradition. What this means will be different for every reader. Indeed, even in the context of single chapters, I found myself questioning or re-evaluating moments of my own life. This book serves; it doesn't feel like filling in multiple-choice questions, staring at a wall of flavorless grocery products, or hearing the endless servant promises of today's political scene. It feels like a humble invitation to consider a single paradoxical element of a profoundly productive tradition.

-Tobias Bates

Acknowledgments

A book on leadership attributes as aspects of Servant Leadership sprouted from the wealth of knowledge and the inspirations of many other leaders. Their writings were sources of inspiration, challenges, and examples of excellence to emulate. I acknowledge the leaders listed below for their help in one way or the other. I am very grateful and I hereby express my appreciation and thanks:

Mr. Wayne Holt, introduced me first to the subject of Servanthood in one of our Stephen Ministerial Training classes, and he is the one who has conducted his life as a leader–servant; he encouraged me throughout my writing;

Dr. Harvey Borovetz, Distinguished Professor and Chair of the Bioengineering Department, is a leader-servant in many ways, he modeled Servanthood and encouragement attributes throughout his leadership in an academic setting.

Dr. Clifford and Dr. Patience Obih, in so many measures exemplified the practical leadership attributes discussed in this book.

Pastor Lance Lecocq, Lead Pastor of Monroeville Assembly of God, for his excellent model of servanthood, empowerment, and emulation attributes to the ministerial team, I am thankful for his motivation and encouragement throughout the several hours on this project;

To my administrative assistant, Ms. Terri Cook, who was always the first to review the manuscript; I am very grateful for her dedication.

To the African Christian Fellowship USA, institutions, and all other organizations where I have served in one leadership capacity or the other, thank you for affording me senior leadership positions that provided the leadership platform and opportunities to grow as a leader.

Dr. Lawrence Owoputi, a brother I am proud to call my friend; for his dedication to serving others, his generosity, healing care, and responsibility attributes during our term in office and in chapter leadership positions; he taught me that excellent following is also part of good leadership;

To Tobias Bates, for his editorial work on the original draft of the book, and his dedication to completing the work.

Mr. Edward F. Kondis, a member of our Engineering Board of Visitors, for his always encouraging and moral support;

Dr. Enefaa N. Wosu, my wife and life partner, for her love, commitment, and prayer support, especially during those long night hours I was not there for her and her constant reminder of who I must be as a leader-servant. Without her support, forbearance, wisdom, and encouragement, this project would not have been completed; I say, thank you very much.

And to God alone be all the glory and honor for the divine inspiration and guidance in initiating and completing this life-transforming book project.

Dedication

I humbly submit this book back unto the gracious hands of God who inspired the writings through His Holy Spirit!

I dedicate this book to my virtuous wife of 45 years, Rev. (Dr.) Enefaa Wosu whose spiritual leadership is an important gateway to our home, and to our four wonderful children—Prof. Eliada Wosu-Griffin EL, HeCareth, Tamuno-Emi, and Chidinma. From them all, I learnt what it meant to be a leader-servant. I could not be blessed with better teachers.

PREFACE

What characteristics did Biblical leaders like the Apostle Paul, Moses, Joshua, and Nehemiah as servants of their people display outwardly that distinguished them from other leaders, both then and now? The Apostle Paul kept his focus to *emulate* Christ and endured all the infirmities and persecutions he suffered to complete his goal to preach the gospel of Jesus Christ. He inspired Timothy and others through his effective *discipleship* leadership to imitate him as he emulated Christ. Moses' outward display of his *trust* in God's power earned him a good level of trust from the people and empowered him for the mission of delivery of God's children from bondage in Egypt; he had to *reproduce* himself in Joshua to complete the mission. But the greatest of them was Jesus Christ, who humbly sacrificed His life to finish the work of redemption. In His *Servanthood*, commitment, and love for the people, He became the ultimate *model* of a leader as a servant to *emulate*.

Let's consider for a moment secular leaders in these current times! For example, think of Henry Ford, who founded the successful Ford Motor Company; Bill Gates who created the global empire that is Microsoft; Albert Einstein, who in many ways is synonymous with a genius for his contributions to modern physics; Abraham Lincoln, remembered as one of the greatest presidents and leaders of United States; and many others like these we cannot mention. What did all these leaders have in common? What propelled them to turn their initial failures or challenges into eventual successes? None had a direct mentor or inherited any fortune from their parents. Nevertheless, they all eventually succeeded. These people can be distinguished from others based on their self-will to succeed, their self-confidence and belief in themselves, their self-determination, and their perseverance, among other characteristics. The distinguishing characteristics displayed externally in service or relationships toward others are the outward functional attributes that define that leader.

Think about yourself as a student, faculty member, or that new executive. What was it that made your journey to success different and even great? Students and colleagues, when they see or hear about my display of what I have referred to as the 'wilderness walk of faith', have asked me to share the critical attitudinal elements that made me remain inwardly resilient and undaunted and yet outwardly joyful in the difficulties I had faced. This book is the result of those reflections. Let me explain one such teaching moment.

Many years ago, sitting in my research lab on a Saturday morning trying to finish writing my dissertation, a fellow graduate student walked into the room to talk with me. He was contemplating terminating his graduate studies. He was a privileged single male student but felt the load was just too much.

"Sylvanus," he asked, with seriousness in his eyes, "your research advisor suggested that I should ask you, 'what is it that makes you tick?'.'What is it about you that makes you joyful and at peace with yourself and determined to finish, no matter the situations and high expectations we face in this department?"

What he asked me were deeply reflective questions, but I was willing and excited to answer them. Even so, before I do, let's look at the context. At that period in my life, I had four little children as a graduate student; in fact, more children than any of the faculties at that time, except for one faculty member who had eight children. I received little or no support from the department. I was then an international alien, did not qualify for financial aid, and was not given any research assistant position. I was, therefore, self-supported with two off-campus part-time jobs. I joked at being a minority of minorities, the only student in the department with such a label,—but I was self-willed to succeed. My adaptability attribute, coupled with perseverance and resilience, was all that I needed to succeed despite the odds against me. In every exam, homework assignment, or project I had to compete with students with full financial aid, plus they had nothing to distract their attention from their studies. I lived with the attitude that using disadvantages as an excuse was not an option. Aspiring to earn my Ph.D. was a life dream, and I was willing to give my ultimate best to actualize that dream even in the face of challenges. The choice was mine!

So I looked at my classmate and all I could see was a student striding through a valley through which I also walked. He needed me to show him how to walk the walk, to empathize with him. To answer his question, I smiled, not that I wanted to, but because it was just who I was. The joy he attributed to me was an overflow of my appreciation of God's grace that His life in me was externally manifesting His light to bless someone else. It was a great teaching moment; I capitalized on it to tell my classmate that my joy was not about me. He could see physically but about He who was in me, he could not see in the flesh; I needed him to know that I was just showing forth His life in me. At first, my classmate did not understand the spiritual prose or metaphor I was using. He looked surprised but open to hearing more.

I did not ask if he was a Christian. However, right on my desk was my small green pocket Bible. I opened to 2 Corinthians 12:9 (NIV) and handed it to him to read. As he read the passage: "But he said to me, 'My grace is sufficient for you, for my power is made perfect in weakness.' Therefore, I will boast all the more gladly about my weaknesses, so that Christ's power may rest on me," I noticed how absorbed he was in the words

He looked astonished and read it again, this time silently. "This is interesting, but what does this mean?" He asked. I took his question to mean, "How does this relate to my question?

I explained to my friend that the external attitudes he or my advisors saw in me that warranted the question, "What makes you tick" were inspired by my inner value system based on my faith in this same Christ and His teachings. My desire to manifest His life and self-confidence is all because of what He has promised in His word if I believed. I have believed His words and have gained self-determination and faith to make the right choices through Him for my life, and his spirit has given me perseverance and resilience to focus on finishing strong in pursuit of any goal. "With that faith, I have continued, more passionately and excitedly; I can look at my challenges and vulnerabilities and delight joyfully in them, even as an alien minority of minorities! His grace and power have empowered me to do all things I want to do. That is what makes me tick," I explained.

He looked at me as if he got his answer. "Wow, thanks!" he said, looking inspired and ready to face his challenges. As we concluded with a prayer, and he stood up to leave, I pointed empathetically to his face and said, "If I made it despite my challenges, you have absolutely no excuse but to persevere to complete your studies; you can make it too!"

It is fitting to report that this encounter with my classmate transformed his will and determination to continue. Yes, he was encouraged and went on to complete his graduate studies. He emulated self-will and perseverance from the example of the most vulnerable of all students in the department.

The inner value system of a Leader-Servant is founded not only on his faith but his self-will, coupled with self-leadership; it is the greatest mentor who can turn any situation into an inconceivable success. Self-will is the primary driver for determination, resilience, and perseverance. It is what wakes you up in the morning to ask for strength to do whatever it is you are setting out to do. Based on my life walk of faith, I can state with absolute certainty that faith is the unseen assuredness that can empower you to turn your life's probable impossibilities into great and improbable possibilities.

ABOUT LEADER AS SERVANT LEADERSHIP (LSL) MODEL

Looking at the testimony above, do you know the source that energizes the characteristics you display outside and how your inner self is related to what others see outside? What distinguishes you from others is what combines to define your attributes! As a follower, can you identify the characteristics that distinguish your leaders? As an executive, how do you base your evaluation of yourself? Or how do you evaluate that brand-new manager or new youth director you want to hire? To what do you compare the individual's qualities when you look at his CV? What is the basis of your measure? Do you know if you are a substantial leader? These personal questions and much more are the subjects of this two-volume book, 'The Authentic Leader as Servant Part I: The Outward Leadership Attributes, Principles, and Practices', is written in two parts; the second part 'The Leader as Servant Leadership Model. Part II'; deals with the Inner Strength Leadership Attributes, Principles, and Practices.

When we think about today's corporate greed, deepening divide between the haves and have-not, gridlock in political systems, conflicts and wars, high divorce rates, and the rich young ruler in the Bible, it is easy to agree that all these people share a few things in common: self-centeredness, pride, lack of compassion, and greed. There is a great need in today's suffering world for leader-servants who display leadership attributes. These attributes should be oriented toward selfless service to others. Indeed, our world is increasingly drifting away from global serving reality toward the self and apathy. The most credible message or model for a possible solution to this dilemma and the answer to several complex leadership questions can be found in the foundation of the ultimate leader-servant, Jesus Christ. This book defines the Leader as Servant Leadership attribute as the combined acts of two or more distinctive functional leadership characteristics exhibited in service and relationship toward others. There is no better time than now for a book that presents comprehensive and irrevocable facts and principles regarding how to develop effective attributes of the leader-servant.

The Leader as Servant Leadership Model

My first book on this subject, The Leader as Servant Leadership Model, explains that Jesus' servant leadership model is based on the notion of a Leader as a Servant and not on a Servant as Leader. There are four distinct differences between a Servant as Leader (Servant-leader) and the Leader as Servant (leader--servant) models. It is pertinent to highlight them here to connect to this book, Authentic Leader as Servant.

A Leader as Servant is a leader first. The leader–servant as a leader does not in the line of duty go projecting or lording his or her power and authority over others but is the person to lead the process of influencing desired changes in others through his humble example of being a servant or having a serviceable attitude toward others. He or she is a serving leader, not a lording leader. He leads as a servant by putting others' needs above his own needs and rights. Jesus emphasized the word "as" meaning that the leader (the Master) chooses to serve as a servant even though he is the leader. A leader–servant emulates Jesus, who gave up all rights, and emptied and expended Himself on His followers. He empowered them to become more like Him. A leader-servant is known as a leader first but is seen as a great leader by his humble attendant heart and acts of service to others. His greatness comes from his ability to put others above himself.

Leader as Servant is a Biblical Concept. The model or image of a humble serving leader motivated Jesus' disciples to see that if their master could do this for them, they must also be able to do it for others. Jesus clearly demonstrated the process of leader-as-servant leadership. In some cases, He chose to serve by leading when He wanted to create the image or model of the leader-servant in certain acts. In other cases, He chose to lead by serving, when he showed care and empathy toward the people and led the disciples to see empathy as a leadership attribute.

Leader as Servant is an Authentic Leadership Model to follow. The Leader as the Servant leadership model intentionally positions Jesus as an original model of a leader to follow.

He was serving His disciples to demonstrate that the process of becoming a great leader was earned through humble acts of service to others; He made them understand that He was empowering them to succeed Him as leader-servants through service to others. The result was an incomparable legacy of leadership that changed their communities. The fact that Jesus relinquished his rights or shared His power did not diminish His power and influence. In fact, his influence increased at least 11 X 100%, if we ignore the one case of Judas.

The Leader as Servant Transforms Organizational Culture. The proposed LSL model seeks to transform and sustain the community or organization by instilling key leadership values or "leadership presence" among followers or an organization's members. Change is sustained when everyone in the organization takes ownership of the change. Rather than focusing on leading more followers to be great followers who conform to the organizational culture, LSL seeks to lead and empower better leaders to be distinguished leaders and community builders.

There are four distinctions, which clearly differentiate many of the existing servants as Leader-based philosophies in relation to servant leadership from my LSL model. Even in the corporate or institutional worlds, there is nothing better than Jesus on which to base Servant Leadership. There is nothing more authentic and impacting than the servant leadership modeled by the life and teachings of Jesus Christ.

The LSL model uses exploratory questions, scenarios, and graphic visualizations to excite critical thinking in ways no other book on this subject has yet attempted. Several personal testimonies of my wilderness walk of faith with God are used to connect the reader to real-life experiences of the concepts discussed. The riveting effect is that the text engages and encourages the reader to walk through the experiences presented. The aim is to inspire the reader spiritually, mentally, and professionally with this far-reaching exposition on the subject of servant leadership.

ABOUT THE AUTHENTIC LEADER AS SERVANT (ALS)

The *Authentic Leader as Servant* argues that no leadership model is as authentic, other-centered, able to build communities, and productive and service-oriented as the model of our ultimate leader-servant, Jesus Christ. No source can provide a better point of reference than that provided in the Bible. Hence, this book aims to be more than just a text on leadership; it hopes to be a personal discovery for those who aspire to develop effective leadership attributes that grow leaders as servants who ultimately develop thriving other-centered communities. This book presents a comprehensive, biblically-based study regarding how to develop these attributes and how they are applied in a servant leadership process. In this biblical context and for clarity, Servant Leadership means *Leader-as-Servant Leadership*. A *leader-servant* refers to a *leader as a servant*, which is distinct from a servant-leader or servant as leader.

Leader as Servant Leadership attributes are shaped by the Leadership's Inner Value system, which consists of character, motivation, and commitment. The *Authentic Leader as Servant* is presented as a necessary resource to complement my *The Leader as Servant Leadership (LSL) Model*. The LSL model integrates a transformative leadership framework and interactive dimensions of Servant Leadership. Leader as Servant Leadership is a process in which a leader, in his leadership position, purposefully chooses to put others' rights and needs above his positional rights and personal needs. He then serves, enables, and empowers followers for growth that builds a thriving organization. The LSL model looks at the predominant Servant Leadership concepts and shares how they compare with biblical principles on how we should lead and be led.

ABOUT THE ALS COURSES

The three books, *LSL Model* and *The Authentic Leader as Servant* (Parts I and II), together demonstrate that with today's global visions to reach people of all races and cultures, now is the time for an authentic servant's heart of service. Those visions and the leadership processes are most effective with the appropriate leadership attributes centered more on people than on the organization, principles regarding how to develop effective attributes of leader-servant.

The ALS I and II combined presented twenty leaders as servant leadership attributes. The series of ALS courses supply training guide to understand, develop, and practice the attributes in a leadership process. Each course is independent and self-contained and does not depend on completing any other course in the series of 20 courses. It is, however strongly recommended, in fact a must read, that chapters 1 and 2 in each series be covered as they lay the foundation of LSL model on which ALS is based.

ALS (Parts I & II) Course Layout

The *Authentic Leader as Servant (ALS)* leadership (parts I and II) book has been broken down into 20 courses in workbook format to achieve three goals 1) Self-discovery of the acts of developing the attribute under review in the course, 2) deeper understanding of the principles, research and biblical teaching behind the attributes, and 3) Learning the strategies for practicing the attributes.

Instruction

The set of questions following each chapter are designed to serve as a guide to discover, explore, and practice the essential ALS leadership attributes, principles, and practices in leadership process. The questions are comprehensive review based on the content of this specific chapter only.

To maximize the learning outcomes, the learner must read through this chapter and sections. Some referenced scriptures in the book are repeated in the summaries for added review if needed, even though they were discussed in the section in which they apply.

> The exercises that follow each chapter will help you in not only understanding your own strength and weaknesses in your acts of the attribute but will guide you in developing practical strategies you can apply in self-leadership process or helping others grow in leadership
>
> All answers to the questions are contained in the associated chapter or sections; consultation of new sources, except for the reference scriptures, is not needed. Thus, it is expected that you answer the questions after you have read the associated section or chapter of the workbook. The scripture or other references cited are only for references as they already discussed in the book

ALS I Course 1: Affection Leadership Attribute—*Affection flows from a person to produce positive emotions for the well-being of another person.*

An average person will define the word "love" in the sense that affection is a characteristic of love. Nevertheless, that definition clouds the functional meaning of affection as an attribute of a leader-servant. Affection is a love action intentionally given to someone to create favorable emotion. We experience a positive emotion when we receive or give affection. In his acts of affection, the Apostle Paul communicated to the Corinthian Christians how he spoke to them freely with an open heart, because it was an important way to give affection (2 Corinthians 6:11-13). He also spoke of longing for them with the affection of Jesus Christ (Philippians 1:8); an affection that needs to be mutual (1 Peter 1:7). How is the affection leadership attribute an outward leadership attribute? This course explores this and other questions to discover the characteristics of affection attributes and to formulate a functional principle based on the expected outcome of affection and the effective use of these attributes in leadership.

ALS I Course 2: Discipleship Leadership Attribute- *Discipleship transforms and empowers followers for service leadership that grows communities.*

Discipleship as an act of developing a follower toward a specific goal is an important function of leadership to equip others to lead. *Discipleship transforms and empowers followers for service leadership that grows communities*. A disciple is a follower who willingly chooses to follow the master and submits to his discipleship and authority. In that regard, Jesus wanted all his followers to be his disciples and ambassadors because a disciple is always a follower. Organizationally, a follower could be a junior employee, any employee in a brand-new department, a new younger faculty, or just any person that needs to be guided through a journey of professional growth and good success. This course focuses on the general growth of followers through the acts of discipleship and presents the critical characteristics of discipleship as a leadership outward attribute. Functional definitions of leadership discipleship attributes and its principle will be presented based on those characteristics. Each characteristic will be discussed in detail with emphasis on strategies of how they can be further developed or practiced as a part of the servant leadership process.

ALS I Course 3: Emulation Leadership Attribute—*A great leader-servant outwardly and positively inspires a pattern of good works for others to follow.*

To emulate is to strive to be like someone else or to follow someone else's example by imitating something that inspires you about that person. This course evaluates how to learn from someone good leadership qualities to develop yours. How did you use what you learned from following the footstep of your hero to grow your leadership qualities. Jesus in the scripture modeled humility and Servanthood he wanted his disciples to develop same qualities. Emulation as a leadership attribute shares some characteristics with transformative leadership, where a leader intentionally conveys a clear vision of a goal, inspires the passion for the work toward the goal, and motivates the followers to follow. As a leader, how do you model a characteristic behavior for someone to follow or develop? How is Leadership Emulation Leadership Attribute an outward leadership attribute? This course explores this and other questions to discover the characteristics of affection attributes and to formulate a functional principle based on the expected outcome of effective use of these attributes in leadership.

ALS I Course 4: Generosity Leadership Attribute: G*enerosity is an outward measure of the level of sacrifice, what is shared, or the impact a giving makes, not just the size of the giving*

Generosity can be defined as "the *habit of giving* without expecting anything in return. It can involve offering time, assets, or talents to aid someone in need." Such habits can include spending your personal money, time, and/or labor for the welfare of others or expending (suffering or being consumed or spending) for others' well-being. When political leaders or Board members 'vote their conscience' on important issues that affect others, what is that "conscience" and how do such leaders contribute to the welfare of others? How can you, "Do all you can, with what you have, in the time you have, in the place where you are" for the betterment of humanity   All giving to help humanity is crucial to help meet the needs of the most vulnerable of God's children, as demonstrated by God as attribute of God, In this course, we will explore what distinguishes a leader's act of giving from his inside intentions. The key leadership characteristics of generosity will be discussed with respect to Servant-Leadership generosity Attributes and Principles and the details how a leader-servant can develop those characteristics and then effectively practice service leadership.

ALS I Course 5: Healing-Care Leadership Attribute: *Comforting others in any trouble with the comfort with which God comforts us, brings healing-wholeness*

What is healing Care and what does it mean in practical terms to you as a leader? Effective leadership begins with an emotionally and spiritually healthy leader who can reconcile and bring comfort to the followers, irrespective of followers' feelings (good or bad) toward the leader. The healing attribute and personal security complement each other. You must have the capacity for self-healing and individual security if you are to meet others' comforts. Personal security provides the infrastructure to support leaders in adversity and heal others that are hurting. A leader's or a group's success is measured by the strength of the weakest member or follower in the group or team… Healing is one of the most abstract and least understood attributes in leadership, and yet one of the most important. The key distinguishing characteristics will be explored to formulate a working definition and principle of leadership healing-care attributes based on those characteristics. Each characteristic will be discussed in detail with emphasis on strategies of how they can be further developed or practiced by a leader-servant as part of the servant leadership process.

ALS I Course 6: Influence Leadership Attribute-*The true measure of leadership success in affecting desired change in conduct, performance, and relational connections in others is influence*

Leadership is an integrative process in which a person applies appropriate (leadership) attributes to guide and influence the desired attitudinal changes in others toward accomplishing a particular goal. Eight five percent of CEOs of top companies surveyed on their climb to leadership ladder said they were "influenced by another leader," compared to 10% and 5% for "natural gifting" and "result of a crisis," respectively. When we consider influence as a servant leadership attribute, we are talking about a distinguishing leadership characteristic that displays on the outside what a leader is inside, influence takes on a deeper meaning. In this course, the key leadership characteristics of influence will be identified and explored from research to frame definitions of the Servant-Leadership influence attribute and principle. Based on those characteristics, the key outcomes of effective leadership influence l how a leader-servant can develop those characteristics and then effectively practice service leadership.

ALS I Course 7: Persuasion Leadership Attribute—*The means of transforming others to a new perspective is through empathetic persuasion.*

Persuasion attribute affords the leader the capacity to convince his followers or others to believe and engage in a new idea or goal through encouragement rather than using his positional authority or intimidation. Because members of the group may already have their views on an issue, the leader must carefully approach persuasion as a learning process to avoid conflicts or polarizing the group. He must unify the diversity of views to get buy-in and willingness to agree and follow. The leader-servant primarily relies on making decisions within an organization based on persuasion rather than positional authority. In other words, you will never hear the Leader-servant say, "Do it because I am the boss, and I say to." This particular element offers one of the clearest distinctions between the traditional authoritarian model of leadership and the concept of Servant leadership. In this course, we will explore the technique of convincing rather than coercing as one of the most effective ways a leader-servant can build consensus within groups. Key characteristics of persuasion leadership attribute will be found, fully discussed, and modeled from the examples in the lives of other leaders.

ALS I Course 8: Reproduction Leadership Attribute—*Great leaders produce successors for legacy and greater courses as an expected product of an effective leadership reproduction.*

In his book, *360 Degree Leader*, John C. Maxwell says, "Great leaders don't use people so they can win. They lead people so they can all lead together." Such great leaders, like Jesus, Moses, Paul, and others developed other leaders through a process of reproduction. Is it possible for leaders of today to reproduce their vision in others so that can lead and build a legacy together? The answer to this question is of course yes. However, the effectiveness of a leader duplicating his leadership qualities in a follower depends on the leadership reproduction attribute of the leader. This course explores the distinguishing characteristics of reproduction as an outward attribute in servant leadership. Functional definitions of leadership reproduction attribute and its principle will be presented based on those characteristics. Each characteristic of reproduction attributes will be discussed in detail with emphasis on strategies of how they can be further developed or practiced by a leader-servant as part of the servant leadership process.

ALS I Course 9: Servanthood Leadership Attribute— *A leader-servant is most qualified to lead when ready to serve as a servant for the growth of others.*

The last time you engaged in a practical act of service on the job, at home, church, or in your community, what were the key elements in that act of service? Did you serve because you wanted to and chose to serve? Or was it because someone asked you to? The ultimate goal is for the leader's life to positively transform many lives in his or her community of followers. Consider the New Testament teachings of Jesus, who demonstrated the ultimate Leader as Servant Leadership. Jesus equated greatness to serving unpretentiously (humbly, as would a child), and He equated leading with choosing to serve others. That is the first affirmative test of authenticity for this attribute. What were the distinguishing characteristics that enabled you to serve? How is the Leadership Servanthood an outward leadership attribute? This course will give answers and meanings to these and personal reflective questions to discover the distinguishing characteristics of The Leadership Servanthood attribute. Functional definitions of The Leadership Servanthood attribute and principle will be provided based on the identified characteristics. Readers will benefit from numerous techniques, personal examples, empirical case study, and applications of the concepts.

ALS I Course 10: Trust-Integrity Leadership Attribute—*True leadership trust produces assured trustee's confidence and readiness to follow based on the credibility, competence, and shared relational connections of the trusted.*

A study examined more than 75 key components of employee satisfaction in top leadership and found that trust and confidence was the single most reliable predictor of employee satisfaction in an organization. This course will examine the results of the above study with respect to servant leadership, and how a leader-servant increases the satisfaction of the followers in an organization. When the organization is going through some challenges, how can a leader be credible in helping the followers understand the company's mission and strategy? How can he share information on how the company or institution, or department is doing and how the followers or employees will be affected? Suppose the organization's strategy is not aligned with its inner value or character, how does the leader build trust in followers or earn trust from them? Organizational leadership trust has been defined by as "an employee's willingness to take a risk for a leader with the expectation that, in exchange, the leader will behave in some desired way." The course will examine how the element of reliance and confidence in the actions of the trusted and organization are characterized by a combination of Competence (Can they do the job?), Benevolence (Do they care about me?), and Integrity (Are they honest?).

Referenced Scriptures

A variety of Bible translations from over 11,200 original Hebrew, Aramaic, and Greek words to about 6,000 English words do exist with variations in meanings and emphases. I am not a biblical scholar and do not pretend to be one; Hence, I have avoided researching the roots of these words and personally prefer New King James Version (NKJV). I have intentionally used other translations for three main reasons; first, to allow for increased impact and alignment of words to the most desired meaning and emphasis in the concepts being addressed. Second, I wanted new and personal discovery of meanings from translations with which I have not been familiar. And third, I wanted to allow readers who may desire translations other than the NKJV the benefit of their preferred translations. Hence, in addition to the NKJV, other translations used in the book include New International Version (NIV), New Living Translation (NLT), King James Version (KJV), English Standard Version (ESV), and Good News Translation (GNT). Unless otherwise specified, NKJV should be assumed.

Sylvanus Nwakanma Wosu

CHAPTER 1
UNDERSTANDING LEADERSHIP ATTRIBUTES

Leadership attribute is the combined acts of two or more distinctive functional leadership characteristics exhibited in service and relationship toward others.

The starting point of our discussion is the understanding of the key functional definitions and concepts that describe the theme of this book. In general, 1 will define leadership as an integrative process in which a person applies appropriate attributes to guide and influence the sought-after attitudinal changes in others toward accomplishing a particular goal. Specifically, the Leader as Servant Leadership is a process in which a leader intentionally chooses to put the follower's rights and needs above his positional rights and personal needs, and serves, enables, and empowers them for desired spiritual and professional growth that builds thriving communities.

FUNCTIONAL DEFINITIONS

In the context of these definitions, I will begin the descriptions of the leadership attributes of an authentic leader-servant by offering a functional definition of Leadership Attributes, and showing how that definition differs from those of Leadership Character, Characteristics, and Traits.

Leadership Character is the sum total of personal qualities in leadership, such as honesty, values, vision, trust, and so on that make up the moral capital of the leader; Leadership character should describe who the leader is inside or the leader's basic personality traits.

The Leadership Characteristics describe the distinctive characteristics or features of a leader, such as attitudes, competencies, skills, and specific experiences that go beyond his character (personality). Leadership characteristics determine how (through skills and competencies) the leader leads or take actions in the process of leadership in any particular situation;

The Leadership traits are the distinguishing leadership characteristics of a leader (these are things that define his leadership characteristics), which differentiate from personality traits... Leadership traits are the set of characteristics that define a particular leader's leadership. This means that a leadership characteristic is a trait when it is a unique characteristic of the leader.

Leadership Attributes, unlike leadership character, characteristics, and traits, is *a leadership attribute and the combined act of two or more distinctive functional leadership characteristics exhibited in service and relationship toward others* or traits externally displayed in action toward others. All leadership attributes grow out of the leadership inner value system but can be externally displayed predominantly as an outbound or outward attribute or both:

1. **Outbound Attributes:** These are distinctive outward-bound attributes emanating from the inner strength of the leader to support external conduct in service and relationships toward others. They form the internal core functional qualities that motivate or enhance the outward manifestation of the inside character toward others. The outbound attribute such as listening and vision, for example, are the direct results of the inner values of the leader such as patience, hearing, love, humility, or all the fruits of the spirit.

2. **Outward Attributes:** These are distinctive functional outward outer visible attributes emanating from the richness of the outbound and inner values of the leader. For example, external attributes such as Servanthood, emulation/modeling, empathy, etc. are outflows from the leader who will directly impact the follower. Outward attributes can be enriched by the outbound (inner) attributes. As shown in Figure 1, the outward attributes in general form the outer core of

CHAPTER 1
UNDERSTANDING LEADERSHIP ATTRIBUTES

functional attributes in the leader as servant leadership, but they can share some overlapping functions with the outbound attributes.

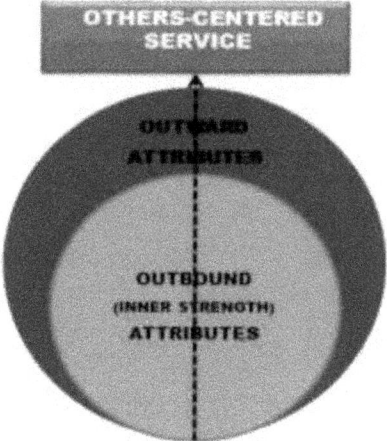

Figure 1.1. Servant leadership functional attributes

In summary, a leadership attribute is more than an ability or a characteristic; it is making those characteristics or abilities functional as part of how the leader acts (his habits) in service to others and applying those characteristics (beyond just having them) in personal and service relations to others. The character or known characteristic defines some aspects of your abilities or who you are inside— e.g. honest, humble, brave, etc. Your attribute, on the other hand, defines your habits; a display of how you use your characteristics, or the actions you exhibit toward others because of who you are inside. For example, empathy as a leadership characteristic becomes a leadership attribute if the followers can distinguish the leader's acts or habits of empathy, such as walking through with his followers in their state of suffering to bring wholeness; otherwise, it is just a characteristic or ability. Leadership attributes toward others are what impact the followers' and the organizational growth more than ability and competence.

In addressing one of the self-righteous hypocritical attributes of servitude leadership, Jesus called leader-servants to be "inside-out" leaders that reflect credibility; indeed, leaders should not appear outwardly righteous when they are full of hypocrisy and lawlessness in their hearts. He was describing "inside–out" as an authentic leadership attribute measured by the display of credibility a leadership attribute!

The measuring stick of a leader-servant is Jesus Christ. We measure ourselves unto the measure of the status of the fullness of Christ (Ephesians 4:13).

The leadership attributes of an authentic leader as a servant are encapsulated in **SERVANT/SERVING LEADERSHIP** are listed in Table 1.1, and defined in Table 1.2: *Servanthood, Emulation, Responsibility, Vision, Navigation, Adaptability, Trust, Listening, Empathy, Affection, Discipleship, Encouragement, Reproduction, Stewardship, Healing-Care, Initiation, Integrity,* and *Persuasion*. Other support attributes include *Influence, Courage, and Generosity.*

The attributes have been separated into Outward and Outbound (Inner Strength) leadership Attributes. As shown in Table 1.1, each of these attributes has three or more leadership characteristics. As such, more than 65 leadership characteristics are covered in these 20 attributes. For example, a leader's Servanthood leadership attribute is characterized by his willing servant's heart of selfless role humility, sacrifice, and submissiveness. The more these are present in a leader, the more effective the servant leadership.

Table 1.1: The functional leader-servant leadership Outbound (Inner Strength) and Outward attributes

	LEADER-SERVANT LEADERSHIP ATTRIBUTES			INNER STRENGTH ATTRIBUTES	OUTWARD ATTRIBUTES
S	Servanthood	L	Listening	Adaptability	Affection
E	Emulation	E	Empathy	Courage	Discipleship
R	Responsibility	A	Affection	Empathy	Emulation
V	Vision	D	Discipleship	Encouragement	Generosity
A	Adaptability	E	Encouragement	Initiation	Healing–Care
N	Navigation	R	Reproduction	Listening	Influence
T	Trust	S	Stewardship	Navigation	Persuasion
I	Influence	H	Healing–Care	Responsibility	Reproduction
G	Generosity	I	Initiation	Stewardship	Servanthood
C	Courage	P	Persuasion	Vision	Trust/Integrity

The list does not assume that a leader has to be excellent in all attributes or even have all of them to be an effective Leader–Servant. However, the more of these attributes the leader displays in his acts of service toward others, the more productive he or she will be, and the further his impact on the followers and organization. The table also shows that two or more attributes can share common characteristics, which can be applied or observed in different contexts. For example, a leader's ability to inspire followers can be seen in his acts of discipleship, empowerment, an.d encouragement attributes in the context in which these attributes apply. Each attribute is exhibited either as a part of the outbound inner strength attribute of a leader or a part of the outward attribute. Table 1.1 is not an exhaustive list of attributes; in fact, there are hundreds of such attributes. This is just the starting point.

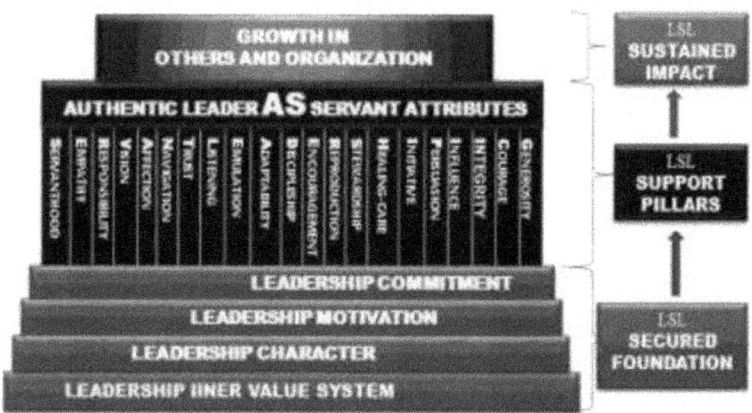

Figure 1.2: Servant leadership outward attributes (dark blue) and relationship to four foundational layers of the LSL Model

Figure 1.2 shows that the leader's attributes are shaped and secured by his four foundational layers (leadership inner value system, leadership character, motivation, and commitment). The attributes of the leader–servants are also conceptualized as the support pillars that will establish and support the personal authenticity of the leader, what the leader, does and the effectiveness of the leadership process. Thus, the attributes represent functional pillars of authentic leadership that can be learned or enriched as described in detail in the subsequent chapters. The combined effect of a secured foundation and stable support pillars will make a sustained impact on the growth of followers and the organization.

COMPARISONS WITH OTHER WORKS

The original works by Greenleaf (1970) in servant leadership [1] have been reviewed by Larry Spears (1996), who identified listening, empathy, healing, awareness, persuasion, conceptualization, foresight, stewardship, commitment to the growth of others, and building community as the ten distinguishing characteristics of servant leadership. [2] Russell (2001) has studied these attributes and have shown them to be essential in servant leadership and concluded that these qualities generally "grow out of the inner values and beliefs of individual leaders." [3] Russell and Stone (2002) extended the Greenleaf 10 attributes to 20 attributes observed in servant-leaders. These 20 attributes were categorized by these authors as either functional attributes (intrinsic characteristics of servant-leaders) or accompanying attributes (complement attributes that enhance the functional attributes).[4] The operational attributes were identified as vision, honesty, integrity, trust, modeling, service, pioneering, appreciation, and empowerment with the accompanying attributes of communication, credibility, competence, stewardship, visibility, influence, persuasion, listening, encouragement, teaching, and delegation. Only three of the attributes identified by Greenleaf were identified, and all three were accompanying attributes rather than functional. Responsibility, adaptability, affection, discipleship, navigation, and reproduction attributes which are considered critical in biblical-based servant leadership in my LSL model are not covered by Russell and Greenleaf. As shown in the description of the attributes in Table 1.2, most of the attributes reported by Russell and Stone (2002)[5] or Greenleaf [1] can be seen either in the twenty attributes or their associated characteristics. Integrity and honesty for example are leadership characteristics of trust and other attributes rather than an independent attributes. I take the position that servant leadership attributes are functional attributes in acts of duty to others and emanate from the inner value system of the leader.

CHAPTER 1
UNDERSTANDING LEADERSHIP ATTRIBUTES

Table 1.2: Description of the functional leader-servant outward leadership attributes and associated principles and characteristics

Leader–Servant Leadership Attributes	Principles of Leadership Attributes	Leadership Characteristics
Affection: *This is the combined love-based works toward providing the essential help or services for the spiritual growth or survival of another person. .* (Chapter 2)	*Affection flows from a person to produce positive emotions for the well-being of another person*	Kindness Compassion Practical Love Affective signs Appreciation
Discipleship: *This is the combined acts of personally developing, intentionally equipping, and attentively empowering growth in others to reproduce a heart of service.* (Chapter 3)	*Discipleship transforms and empowers followers for service leadership that grows communities.*	Inspiring Shepherding Equipping Developing Empowering
Emulation: *This is the combined acts of initiating an authentic servant attitude as a model of service worthy of following* (Chapter 4)	*A great leader-servant outwardly and positively inspires a pattern of good works for others to follow.*	Inspiration Motivation Initiation Model Following
Generosity: *This is the combined acts of freely sharing with and giving to others as an act of kindness, without expectation of reward or return to him.* (Chapter 5)	*Generosity is an outward measure of the level of sacrifice, what is shared, or the impact a giving makes, not just the size of the giving.*	Sharing Giving Kindness Affection Love
Healing-Care: *This is the combined acts of providing comfort and empathy to make others whole emotionally and spiritually along with tending to the follower's physical and mental well-being.* (Chapter 6)	*Comforting others in any trouble with the comfort with which we are comforted by God, brings healing - wholeness.*	Self- Healing Empathy Reconciliation Comfort Relational
Influence: *This is the combined acts of positively affecting desired change in conduct,*	*The true measure of leadership success in affecting*	Model Positive attitude Authority

ALS Servanthood Leadership
Attributes, Principles, & Practices

performance, and relational connections toward others-centered course of action or service. (Chapter 7)	*desired change in conduct, performance, and relational connections in others is influence*	Connection Wisdom Intelligence,
Persuasion: *This is the combined acts of communicating perspective to connect, challenge, and convince with a compelling purpose to convert others to a new position.* (Chapter 8)	*The means of transforming others to a new perspective is through empathetic persuasion*	Connecting Challenging Communicating Convincing Converting Encouraging
Reproduction: *This is the combined acts of developing your leadership qualities in others and releasing them as successors to continue a greater mission.* (Chapter 9)	*Great leaders produce successors for legacy and greater courses as an expected product of an effective leadership reproduction.*	Selecting Mentoring Equipping Empowering Releasing
Servanthood: *This is the combined acts of humility, willingness, and intentionality in service to others through selfless sacrifice and submission as a servant.* (Chapter 10)	*A leader-servant is most qualified to lead when most ready to serve as a servant for the growth of others. The role of a leader is to serve as a servant*	Servant's heart Humility Sacrifice Service Willingness Submissiveness
Trust: *This is the combined acts of positive display of character, competence, credibility, and shared relational connections that produce assured trust-confidence of the trustee in the trusted.* (Chapter 11)	*True leadership trust produces assured trustee's confidence and readiness to follow based on the credibility, competence, and shared relational connections of the trusted.*	Character Competence Integrity Credibility Confidence

Principle of Leadership Attribute

In the context of servant leadership, a leadership attribute is a level above the leadership characteristic or trait of a leader. The principle of leadership attribute states that every leadership attribute has a set of distinguishing characteristics that make up the inward or outward display of the attribute. The principle reflects the essential designed purpose or outcome of the attribute or the inevitable consequence of the effective practice of the attribute. Thus, the principle of leadership attribute is a concise statement about the fundamental truth, value, or belief about the attribute in a leadership situation; it is a statement that establishes an idea about the outcome of the attribute for guiding the practical application of the attribute and its characteristics. I will postulate and frame each principle as an additive function of the characteristics of the attribute. A statement of each principle is quoted at the beginning or below the title of each chapter. It is yet to be experimentally proven if the attribute is a linear or some other non-linear function of these characteristics as variables. It is expected, however, that each character will contribute to the effectiveness of the attribute in varying degrees.

AUTHENTIC LEADERSHIP ATTRIBUTES

At a personal level, attributes are the value-based inside-out moral leadership assets that can be related to the authenticity of a leader-servant. The complexity of defining authenticity has been noted in the literature. The subject of authentic leadership is well covered in the works of Terry (1993),[5] George (2003),[6] and Shair and Eilam (2005).[7] All appear to agree that authenticity requires self-awareness and objective self-identity in personal and social interactions with others. In his book, *Advocacy Leadership*, Professor Gary L. Anderson offers individual, organizational, and societal perspectives on authenticity: "Authenticity, at a peculiar level, is living a life, whether in the private or professional term. This is congruent with one's espoused values; at the structural level, authenticity has to do with viewing human beings as ends in themselves, rather than means to other ends; at the public level, it is a state of affairs that is congruous with the shared political and cultural values of society."[8]

The basic tenets of these perspectives are very fitting to authenticity as a qualifying element of leader-servant leadership attributes. The attribute reflects how the followers see the leader based on the leader's distinctive features displayed through his or her actions personally, organizationally, and societally. The leader is seen as a leader-servant or serving leader because the followers see him lead as a servant from an inside-out value of others. This is what makes the leader authentic. Authenticity means that what a leader displays outside, in personal or leadership life of service to others, and society is based on the values the leader espouses inside.

Authenticity in servant leadership can be one or two types or both: *Outbound Authenticity and Outward Authenticity*. The Outbound (outward-bound) Authenticity is the genuineness of personal honesty from your inner strength and abilities; what you say and how you act emanate from who you are or how you feel inside. It reflects the essential truth and honesty about your outward-bound inner strength.

Outward authenticity, on the other hand, describes the truthfulness of your credibility and honesty displayed outward in relation to others; your *outer* visible behavior or how you act outwardly towards others reflects exactly your true intentions.

While *outward* authenticity is the visible *outer* indicator of the truth of who you are inside, *outbound* authenticity is outward-bound attribute from the inside of who you are. Credibility in this context is the influence a leader has to attract believability, trustworthiness, and authenticity; it is the believability, trustworthiness, and authenticity of who you are inside and outside.

A key element of personal authenticity is that it is seen or measured in the context of societal, cultural, and organizational interactions. In that context, achieving individual authenticity becomes a challenge since it is influenced by social factors and dispositions of individuals who usually depend on liberal and organizational realities. However, for leader-servant leadership, the leader can face those changing times by remaining focused on his key Biblical-based principles or *Leadership Inner Value System*. Thus, I am interested in authenticity as an essential element of effective Leader-servant leadership attributes or Leader-servant leadership attributes as drivers of leadership authenticity. With that in mind, the first critical element of authenticity in practicing or developing efficient leader-servant leadership attributes is inside-out self-examination relative to the people served rather than the organization. You may ask yourself: What will be my response when the people I lead act or react in a certain way, will it be negative or positive? What are my strengths and vulnerabilities at those times?

Professor Yacobi in his post, "Elements of Human Authenticity," noted that since "the self -arise attribute emerges from interactions between self, others, and the environment in a complex society and world, there may co-exist multiple complicated identities depending on place and context." [9] He went on to identify the following <u>essential elements of personal authenticity</u>: self-awareness, unbiased self-examination, accurate self-knowledge, reflective judgment, personal responsibility, and integrity, genuineness, and humility, empathy for others, understanding of others, optimal utilization of feedback from others. All of these are covered under the leadership attributes or characteristics shown in Table 1.2.

Bill George, in his book, *Authentic Leadership*, takes the position that to be an authentic leader; a person must have the following essential characteristics: [10]

- Behavior based on value: He must understand his own values and exhibit behavior to others based on those values;
- He must not compromise his values in difficult situations but could use the situation to strengthen personal values in those situations.
- Passion from a clear purpose: Be self-aware of who he is, where he is going, and the right thing to do.
- Compassion from the heart: He must lead from a compassionate heart that allows them to be sensitive to the plight and needs of others,
- Connectedness from a relationship; he must be relationally connected with people he leads,
- Consistency from the self-disciple: He must demonstrate self-discipline to remain calm, collected, and consistent in a stressful situation.

Modeled after the elements above, Table 1.3 lists six essential characteristics of authenticity for servant leadership. These fundamental characteristics cover the five identified above and can also be aligned with the leadership characteristics in Table 1.2. Each attribute in Table 1.2 is expected to pass the personal authenticity test in Tables 1.3, 1.4. In a survey of 132 Christian leaders, seventy-four percent (74%) of them agreed that they always or frequently exhibit servant leadership attributes. [11] Thus, a pass of the outward authenticity test means that a pure leader must demonstrate 70% or more of these essential elements of this legitimacy. (That is, 70% YES in the assessment questions in Tables 1.3, 1.4).

It needs to be noted, however, that a secular leader could be authentic and still lack some of the essential servant leadership attributes or characteristics such as selflessness, servanthood, and love-motivated servant attitudes of a leader-servant. Effective leader-servants are authentic leaders and personal authenticity is an essential element of leader-servant leadership. The key test for leader-servant authenticity is the quality of his inside-out value and personal character. What is most important is a change from the inside-out.

	Table 1.3: The test of essential elements of personal inner strength authenticity in servant leadership		
	Elements of Inner Strength Authenticity	**Inner Strength (Outbound) Authenticity Assessment Questions**	**YES / NO**
1	Personal inside-out value-based behavior	Are your personal inside-out values aligned with acts of service and behavior outside?	1
		Are you honest to yourself in relation to your inner strengths and abilities?	2
2	Inside-out Self-Awareness	Do you have unbiased self-examination, and accurate self-knowledge of who you are inside-out?	3
		Do you know your inner strength and weaknesses in relation to the good you want to show as an outward attribute?	4
3	Inside-out Empathy-Compassion	Do you know and feel from your inside what you want for your followers?	5
		Are you motivated to empathize, based on your inside feelings?	6
4	Inside-out Connection with followers	Do you feel deep, personal, and spiritual connection with your followers?	7
		Does what you say and how you act reflect how you feel when you relate to others?	8
5	Inside-out Emotional Self-regulation	Do you have difficulty controlling your emotion in order to remain calm in a stressful situation?	9
		Are you always able to comfort yourself?	10
6	Inside-out Authenticity Feedback	Do your followers see your inside-out value from your outside behavior?	11
		Will your followers feel that what you say you are is congruent with how you act?	12
	#YESs_____; # NOs_____: Outbound Authenticity: YES/ 12----------%		

Table 1.4: The test of essential elements of personal outward authenticity in servant leadership

	Elements of Personal Outward Authenticity	Personal Outward Authenticity Assessment Questions	YES or NO
1	Personal value-based outward behavior	Are your personal values and beliefs aligned with your acts of service and behavior toward others?	1
		Do you live out your life according to your beliefs?	2
2	Personal Self-Awareness	Do you have clarity of your personal vision and purpose?	3
		Does what you know about yourself accurately describe what others say?	4
3	Personal Outward Empathy-Compassion	Do you apply how you feel to what your followers need?	5
		Do you lead from a compassionate heart and are you sensitive to the plight and needs of others?	6
4	Personal Connection with followers	Do you feel deep, personal connection with your followers?	7
		Does your outward action toward others reflect exactly your true intentions?	8
5	Outward Emotional Self-regulation	Do you have difficulty controlling your emotions to remain calm in a stressful situation?	9
		Does your evaluation of your value of others agree with how valued they feel?	10
6	Personal Authenticity Feedback	Do your followers see your outward acts as true and honest?	11
		Can your followers see other-centeredness in 70% or more of your attributes?	12

#YESs_____ ; # NOs_____ ; Outward Authenticity: YES/ 12----------%

ALS SERVANTHOOD LEADERSHIP
ATTRIBUTES, PRINCIPLES, & PRACTICES

Table 1.5. Leader As Servant-Leadership Audit

A servant-leader in his leadership position purposefully choses to serve and inspire acts of service in others by his example. Select and circle best answer to questions
1=Never: 2=Almost never ; 3=Sometimes; 4=Frequently; 5 =Always

	Servant Leadership assessment questions	Circle no				
1	I am willing and other-centered, and readily chose to serve others as a servant for their personal growth	1	2	3	4	5
2	I model others-centered attitude in my service and relationships and inspire same for others to follow	1	2	3	4	5
3	I have a sense of obligation, willingness, and accountability for the service towards others	1	2	3	4	5
4	I have the foresightedness to specify in the present view what others' growth should be in a given future	1	2	3	4	5
5	I work toward providing the essential help or services for the spiritual growth or survival of the others;	1	2	3	4	5
6	I provide the needed purposeful course of action for how to chart the course to for my followers.	1	2	3	4	5
7	I display external credibility and a strong sense of character based on values, beliefs, and competence;	1	2	3	4	5
8	In communication, I attentively perceive and hear what is communicated, reflectively listen to understand and to be understood	1	2	3	4	5
9	I walk through with others in their state (suffering, emotions, etc.) in a way that provides the needed care and well-being	1	2	3	4	5
10	I have a measure of self-secured flexibility to adapt appropriate attitude to serve all people in different situations	1	2	3	4	5
11	I personally develop, intentionally equip, and attentively nurture spiritually growth in others	1	2	3	4	5
12	My act of bravery instills in others the courage and confidence to follow or persevere in a course of action	1	2		4	5
13	I develop my leadership qualities in others as successors to continue in a purposeful mission	1	2	3	4	5
14	I manage , maintain,, and account for all resources entrusted to me and being responsible for the difference my acts make	1	2	3	4	5
15	As a care-giver, I act to comfort and make others whole emotionally	1	2	3	4	5
16	When I see a need, I originate a vision and action, and stay committed to meet that need and desired change	1	2	3	4	5

Chapter 1
Understanding Leadership Attributes

17	I display a holistic view of an issue to inform, transform or convert others to my view through empathetic persuasion	1	2	3	4	5
18	I freely share what I have sacrificially as an act of kindness to others, without expectation of reward in return	1	2	3	4	5
19	My act of influence is to affect the actions, behavior, opinions, etc., of others based on trust, credibility and relationship	1	2	3	4	5
20	In the face challenges and danger, I act with bravery to overcome fear and take a stand with strength and conviction	1	2	3	4	5
Score Range	Add up the numbers in each column (Total Score____ Check and Understand the key areas to work on					
81-100	Strong Leader-Servant; keep it up, go and train others.					
66-80	Above average Leader-Servant; work 25% of key areas					
50-65	Average but developing; need to work on 50% of key areas					
34-49	Below average leader; work on 75% of key areas					
<34	Not a Leader-Servant; need training in all areas					

Summary 1
Understanding Leadership Process

Before starting this exercise, please read and follow the instruction in the preface of this workbook. Answers to these questions are contained in this chapter. Completion of these exercises after reading the chapter should take 60-90 minutes.

Discovering the Leadership Attributes

1. What is your alternative definition of leadership? In learning to lead, how would you differentiate the following elements:
    a. Leadership,
    b. Leader as servant leadership.
    c. Leadership characteristics.
    d. Leadership attributes
2. How should you lead in the context of this chapter?

Understanding the Leadership Principles

1. Define or state the principle of Servanthood Leadership attribute. How true is that in your leadership experience?
2. What are the key differences between the Leader as Servant and the Servant as Leader Leadership philosophies?
3. How can you display the essential qualities of authentic leader in a leadership process in challenging times.?
4. What are the characteristics of a leader-servant?
5. What was the original source of the Servant as Leader (SL)? What was the original source of Leader as Servant (LS)?
6. How do you compare the two model characters of Leo in SL and Jesus in LS
7. What is the key framework of a Leader as a Servant Leadership?

Practicing Authentic Leadership

1. Authenticity in servant leadership can be one or two types or both *Outbound Authenticity and Outward Authenticity*: Describe a time when you displayed:
    a. The Outbound (outward-bound)— *outbound* authenticity is outward-bound attribute from the inside of who you are.
    b. *The Outward Authenticity—outward* authenticity is the visible *outer* indicator of the truth of who you are inside,
2. Describe the key elements of personal authenticity seen or measured in the context of societal, cultural, and organizational interactions.
3. Take the outbound (Table 1.3) and Outward (Table 1.4) leadership authenticity tests. How (%) authentic are you (#YES/12) in each measure in your leadership process?
4. In the elements you rated as NO, review the relevant passage, learn what is missing in you and write a personal commitment statement on how to work to improve in those areas
5. How much of a leader-servant are you? Take the personal leader-servant audit in Table 1.5 to self-assess your effectiveness.
6. Based on the questions in Table 1.5, can you identify each of the twenty attributes? What ones did you score 3 ("sometimes") or less than 3? Review and learn and commit to work to improve.

CHAPTER 2
CHARACTERISTICS OF SERVANTHOOD LEADERSHIP ATTRIBUTE

A leader-servant is most qualified to lead when ready to serve as a servant for the growth of others.

The last time you engaged in a practical act of service on the job, at home, church, or in your community, what were the key elements in that act of service? Did you serve because you wanted to and chose to serve? Or was it because someone asked you to? What were the distinguishing characteristics that enabled you to serve? How is the Leadership Servanthood an outward leadership attribute? This chapter will attempt to give answers and meanings to these and personal reflective questions to discover the distinguishing characteristics of The Leadership Servanthood attribute. Functional definitions of The Leadership Servanthood attribute and principle will be provided based on the identified characteristics. Readers will benefit from numerous techniques, personal examples, empirical case study, and applications of the concepts.

CHARACTERISTICS OF SERVANTHOOD ATTRIBUTE

There are several examples of leaders in the Old and New Testaments of the Bible that exemplified the Servanthood attribute. Consider the New Testament teachings of Jesus, who demonstrated the ultimate Leader as Servant Leadership. On this subject, Jesus said; "... But whoever desires to become great among you, let him be your servant. And whoever desires to be first among you, let him be your slave—just as the Son of Man did not come to be served, but to serve, and to give His life a ransom for many" (Matthew 20:26-28) and "He who is greatest among you, let him be as the younger, and he who governs as he who serves. For who is greater, he who sits at the table, or he who serves? Is it not he who sits at the table? However, I am among you as the One who serves" (Luke 22:24-28). These two scriptures offer a powerful explanation of Servanthood. Jesus equated greatness to serving unpretentiously (humbly, as would a child), and He equated leading with choosing to serve others. That is the first affirmative test of authenticity for this attribute.

The leader must be unpretentiously true to his acts of service and not accomplishment by compulsion. Leadership in Jesus' example is helping others as a servant. Although in the Bible being a servant or a slave is used interchangeably, a slave is a lower form of being a servant. An attendant and slave both solely serve or work for a master. A servant has more choice to stay and serve and is not under bondage to a service obligation. A slave, on the other hand, is owned by the master and is under bondage to the service obligation. Thus, a slave is not only a servant but a property or possession of the master's use as he sees fit. Jesus' emphasis on "as" in the above scriptures means that a leader-servant himself chooses to obligate himself to serve others.

The ultimate goal is for the leader's life to positively transform many lives in his or her community of followers. This is the essence of what the Apostle Paul articulated in Corinthians and how he lived by the example of Jesus, "Though I am free and belong to no one, I have made myself a slave to everyone, to win as many as possible. I have become all things to all people so that by all imaginable means, I might save some" (1 Corinthians 9:19-23, NIV).

PRINCIPLE OF LEADERSHIP SERVANTHOOD ATTRIBUTE

From the above scriptures and others, the distinguishing servant leadership servant hood attribute can be identified as acts of servant, sacrifice, humility, and duty. My functional definition is as follows:

Servant Leadership Servanthood Attribute is the combined acts of humility, willingness, and intentionality in service to others through selfless sacrifice and submission as a servant.

CHAPTER 2
SERVANTHOOD LEADERSHIP ATTRIBUTE

Leadership Servanthood Attribute drives a leader-servant to humbly, willingly, and intentionally put the rights of others above his or her rights and choose to serve them.

The outcome of the Servanthood attitude is a selfless readiness for acts of service for the well-being of others. Servant leadership Servanthood principle is defined as follows: A leader-servant is most qualified to lead when ready to serve as a servant for the growth of others. The role of a leader is to serve as a servant.

The sum effect of the leadership Servanthood attribute is expressed as a function of the leadership Servanthood characteristics:

SERVANT + SACRIFICE + SERVICE = SERVANTHOOD

Figure 2.1 illustrates the process of Servanthood, showing that a servant, through humility and obedience, willingly provides acts of service to others because of his love and obedience to the call for good works.

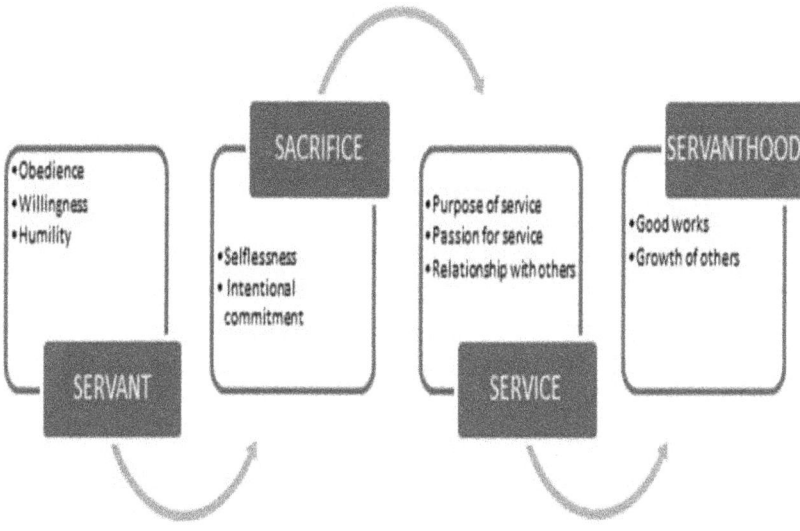

Figure 2.1: Three-stage process of Servanthood

SUMMARY 2
SERVANTHOOD LEADERSHIP ATTRIBUTE

Before starting this exercise, please read and follow the instruction in the preface of this workbook. Answers to these questions are contained in this chapter. Completion of these exercises after reading the chapter should take 60-90 minutes.

Discovering the Leadership Principles

1. List the key elements in your act of service? Did you serve because you wanted to and chose to serve?
2. What are the distinguishing characteristics that enables a leader to serve?
3. Discuss how the Leadership Servanthood is an outward leadership attribute?

Understanding the Principle of Servanthood Leadership Attributes

1. Define or state the principle of Servanthood Leadership attribute. How true is that in your leadership experience?
2. How did Jesus exemplify the Servanthood attribute in the bible when He said, "... But whoever desires to become great among you, let him be your servant. And whoever desires to be first among you, let him be your slave—just as the Son of Man did not come to be served, but to serve, and to give His life a ransom for many" (Matthew 20:26-28) and "He who is greatest among you, let him be as the younger, and he who governs as he who serves. For who is greater, he who sits at the table, or he who serves? Is it not he who sits at the table? However, I am among you as the One who serves" (Luke 22:24-28).
3. The goal in a leader's life is to positively transform many lives in his or her community of followers. How dis Apostle Paul articulated in (1 Corinthians 9:19-23, NIV).

Practicing Servanthood Leadership

1. What does Leadership Servanthood Attribute drive a leader-servant to do?
2. What are some of the outcomes of such acts of servanthood attribute?
3. How can the sum effect of the leadership Servanthood attribute be expressed

CHAPTER 3
DEVELOPING THE SERVANT'S HEART IN SERVANTHOOD

A servant is a subordinate whose primary duty is to serve a master; a person employed by someone to perform a duty. The term servant is used several times both in the old and New Testaments in reference to being a servant of God or servant of fellow human beings. We must recognize that we are servants of the Lord. The word serving in the Bible is a verb form of the Greek noun *doulos*, which means "a slave who has no rights of his own." The ultimate desire of a humble servant is to serve the Lord by serving others. In reference to the action or the act of serving God, each of the most notable leaders in the Old Testament, including Abraham (Genesis 26:24), Moses (Joshua 1:2, 7; 24:29), and David (Jeremiah 33:21-23), as well as others were designated by God as "my Servant." Jesus is the ultimate example of what a leader-servant is and what the act of serving means. He is also the perfect example of what it means to be one who serves others and puts the needs of others above His own. Jesus, in teaching his disciples the act of Servanthood reminded them that, "If He, the Lord and the Teacher, washed their feet, they, furthermore, ought to wash one another's feet" (John 13:12-14). A servant, in his acts of duty, pushes for no rights of his own but advocates for the rights and benefits of the master or others. At the level of serving, though free from the commitment the servant makes himself completely obligated to serve.

In our Stephen Ministry[1], in the Monroeville Assembly of God, we were blessed to have Wayne Holt as one of our Stephen Ministry's. Leaders lay Christian leaders who work together with the pastors as a team to lead Stephen's Ministry. Wayne, in fact, first inspired my deep interest in the subject of servant leadership. Lay Christians receive

---

[1]Stephen Ministry is a one-to-one caring ministry that trains lay caregivers, called Stephen Ministers, equips and empowers them to provide needed care and compassion to the community inside and outside the church

intensive training to be commissioned as Stephen Ministers. As we covered the lesson on Servanthood, I was motivated not only by his organizational skills and outstanding teaching abilities but his down-to-earth humility and servant spirit. Wayne made me begin to think about what it means to lead by serving others. I observed him willingly get involved in numerous church activities. In every situation, you could literally feel the passion and satisfaction with which he served. Be it in singing ministry, organizing a mission trip, or leading the Stephen Ministry, you could see that Wayne chooses to serve others. He gave his full and joyful attention to service. It was as if he derived energy from his busy schedule. One day, I asked him what drove him. Wayne summarized his leader's passion this way: "When you serve because you want and choose to serve, it is like a consuming driver." That comes from the heart of a leader-servant!

Serving is distinctive when you are in a ministry that you do not like or don't want to do. A Christian brother who served as a board member of a church shared with me how he served under the leadership of two different leaders. With the first leader, regular board meetings involved the members sitting down and taking notes. "I did not know what to expect," he shared. "We as members just sat and received information and directions—what to do, how to do it, when to do it, and so on, from the leader. It was more about how to manage the church's resources," the brother recalled. This was simply a one-way, power-control style of leadership. He confessed that he was not happy. When the first leader retired, he was replaced by a second leader who modeled the team concept of leadership. This new leader, according to the brother, would introduce an issue and simply allow members to discuss, contribute, and agree on a consensus. Board members watched this fresh leader serve others and treat everyone as important—if not more valuable than himself. The new leader was a good example of a leader-servant.

Jesus shows that desiring to lead is submitting to serving others, which is as a servant. An effective servant has three key characteristics: *humility, submission,* and *willingness,* motivated by love for others, irrespective of the positions of the persons being served. Jesus knew that Judas would betray him. However, He served Judas by washing his feet. How many modern leaders would serve an enemy that they knew was about to betray or kill them? A helper's obedience to serve others can determine the depth of his sacrifice and commitment to service. One

CHAPTER 3
DEVELOPING THE SERVANT'S HEART IN SERVANTHOOD

can serve by obeying in a "mechanical" way but still lack the humility to effectively choose the lower position of acting willingly as a servant. One can also be humble and obedient but may not have the commitment and willingness to go the extra mile needed in servant leadership.

When the mindset of the leader is that the service, he or she performs is unto God, then true Servanthood emerges. It involves willingly serving the Lord by serving others. What makes Servanthood humbling, yet a privileged experience is that Jesus had no inhibitions concerning such services. He deliberately chose to become a servant of all even though He was God. None are higher than the Divine and yet Jesus became the lowest, a servant, even to His death on the cross.

The three key attitudes or characteristics of a servant: *humility, obedience,* and *willingness* the service others are modeled in Figure 3.1 as an interconnected overlapping relationship:

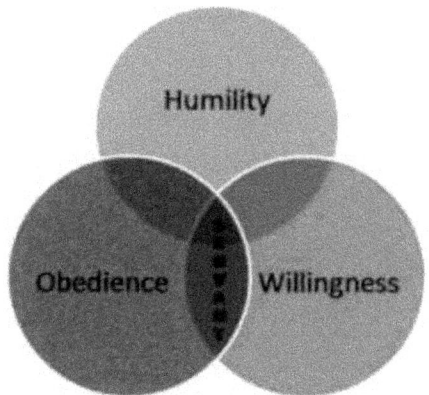

Figure 3.1. Overlapping and interconnected model
Characteristics of a servant in Servanthood attribute

Developing the Acts of the Servant-Humility

Servant-humility is an essential personal humble disposition displayed in actions and attitude in a way that brings him to an equal level with others and meets them on a fair playing ground. This could mean adapting to connecting to the other's culture and finding different ways of serving a need.

A servant's humility is the starting point for the act of Servanthood; it is critical for any successful leader. The true meaning of humility can be understood from Jesus' teaching. Jesus said:

"Therefore, whoever humbles himself as this little child is the greatest in the kingdom of heaven" (Matthew 18:4, NKJV). The "little child" in a leader is the fact that he is humble, unpretentious, meek, and does not seek his pride, even when reviled. Jesus demonstrated the acts of humility via an analogy to a little child and in His washing of the disciples' feet. A humble leader may be great in many things but still, be able to acknowledge his weaknesses without pushing for his positional rights. Jesus' type of meekness and quiet confidence without promoting himself is at the core of humility. The Bible tells us; "Who is wise and understanding among you? Let him show by good conduct that his works are done in the meekness of wisdom" (James 3:13, NKJV)"Therefore, as the elect of God, holy and beloved, put on tender mercies, kindness, humility, meekness, longsuffering" (Colossians 3:12, NKJV). From these examples, we can define personal humility as acting or thinking in a way that does not project oneself as better or more important than others. His humility leads him to obey, and, in doing so, to make a sacrifice of his pride and rights. Let us consider each of the characteristics or attitudes of a servant toward service. These characteristics can be considered secondary attributes of Servanthood in servant leadership.

Humility sets the mind of a leader on the needs of others

A humble leader-servant sets his mind on the needs of others above his rights and position. He humbles himself, and by developing appropriate attributes based on a sound foundation, chooses to sacrifice individual rights to serve others and inspires them to gain more rights and personal growth. For example, Jesus clearly showed that humility is not a sign of weakness but a source of strength for a leader. It is a mark of authenticity and pragmatism without which there would be no empathy and willingness to serve. Humility allows a leader to admit his weaknesses and show his own need for renewed power. We see in Paul the attitude of humility when he defended his teaching and leadership to the Church in Corinth in the midst of false teaching and doctrines, spiritual immaturity, and carnality (2 Corinthians 1-12). Paul responded with absolute humility, without defending himself or the accusations or rationalizing his feelings. Instead, he redirected his energy to bringing a culture of responsibility and personal rebukes and honestly pleading and sharing his heart. As with Jesus' example, Paul saw the work as much more important than himself. Leader-servants humble themselves enough to see the broader perspective and see their wrongs without projecting their self-worth, defending their moves, or making excuses for their failures. Only self-effaced leaders and see beyond themselves without feeling trampled. Setting the mind on the needs of others is to have the attitude to want to serve to please God rather than man. We can develop such an attitude by the following two simple acts:

Understand that our competence is in God and not in ourselves. A feeling that one's competence comes from God removes the temptation to boast about what one feels he is. Paul says that our sufficiency is from God, who has made us sufficient as ministers: "Such confidence we have through Christ before God. Not that we are competent in ourselves to claim anything for ourselves, but our competence comes from God" (2 Corinthians 3:4-5, NIV) Most acts of pride in leaders emerge from feeling self-righteousness or a better-than-thou attitude that often results in impatience and mistreatment of others. Some leaders, on the other hand, beat up themselves for mistakes with the feeling that "I am not supposed to make such mistakes." This also qualifies as a sense of pride, because we are not perfect. When leaders cultivate the sense that competence is really from God, they develop the attitude of humility. It also helps the leader stop thinking that he or she is never good enough. Of course, you will never be enough! You will never be perfect, no matter how you try.

Leave our accomplishments behind and focus on our calling. A feeling that one's competence comes from God removes the temptation to boast about what one feels he is. Paul says that our sufficiency is from God, who has made us adequate as ministers: "Such confidence we have through Christ before God. Not that we are competent in ourselves to claim anything for ourselves, but our competence comes from God" (2 Corinthians 3:4-5, NIV) Most acts of pride in leaders emerge from feeling self-righteousness or a better-than-thou attitude that often results in impatience and mistreatment of others. Some leaders, on the other hand, beat up themselves for mistakes with the feeling that "I am not supposed to make such mistakes." This also qualifies as a sense of pride, because we are not perfect. When leaders cultivate the sense that competence is really from God, they develop the attitude of humility. It also helps the leader stop thinking that he or she is not at any time good enough. Of course, you will not at any time be sufficient on your own! You will never be perfect, no matter how you try.

Leave our accomplishments behind and focus on our calling. Paul said, "Not that I have already obtained all this, or have already arrived at my goal, but I press on to take hold of that for which Christ Jesus took hold of me. But one thing I do: Forgetting what is behind and strain toward what is ahead. I press on toward the goal to win the prize for which God has called me heavenward in Christ Jesus" (Philippians 3:12-14, NIV). In other words, discover what you want in your calling. To Paul, it was Christ's righteousness rather than his; it was to please Christ and complete His agenda. Once you know what is most important, and then focus on how to accomplish that purpose to please God. Paul's attitude was to forget the past, good and bad, accomplishments, his rights, and all things he desired; he did not allow them to distract him. He passionately pressed on toward the goal to win the eternal prize of his calling.

With respect to service, and drawing on concepts from Stephanie Slamka's essay, "Humility as a Catalyst for Compassion"[13] the following can be noted about humility as a critical element of the Servanthood attitude:

- Humility is the way we serve others and our reality. It is what links us to oneness, equality, nothingness, and divinity all at once.
- Humility assists our reception in empathy by helping us to see the other person's need to be served.
- Humility gets us out of our personal minds, out of our individual ego, and our own perceptions long enough to let us see, hear, and sense what others feel and suffer.
- Humility helps us to self-regulate the verbal and nonverbal behaviors in interpersonal relationships in service to others, allowing our self-reflection to be deeper and more accurate.
- Humility allows us to recognize others and see them as equals; it allows us to be open-minded, decrease our sense of pride, and serve others by listening.

SUMMARY 3
DEVELOPING THE SERVANT'S HEART IN SERVANTHOOD ATTRIBUTE

Before starting this exercise, please read and follow the instruction in the preface of this workbook. Answers to these questions are contained in this chapter. Completion of these exercises after reading the chapter should take 60-90 minutes.

Discovering Servant in Servanthood

1. How do you define a servant in service? What does it mean to you to be a servant? What makes you believe you have the qualities of a servant?
2. How was servant's heart in servanthood demonstrated in the lives of notable leaders in the bible including
   a) Abraham (Genesis 26:24),
   b) Moses (Joshua 1:2, 7; 24:29),
   c) David (Jeremiah 33:21-23), as well as others designated by God as "my Servant."
   d) Or by Jesus, the ultimate example of what a leader-servant is and what the act of serving means.?

Principle in act of servant Servanthood Attribute

1. How did Jesus demonstrate act of servant in the passage, "If He, the Lord and the Teacher, washed their feet, they, furthermore, ought to wash one another's feet" (John 13:12-14).
2. Jesus shows as a principle that desiring to lead is submitting to serving others as a servant. What are the three key characteristics of an effective servant: *humility, submission,* and *willingness,*

Practicing acts of a Servant in Servanthood

1. What is the primary motivator of a servant's hearts of service ?
2. When the mindset of the leader is that of service, he or she performs it as unto God, then true Servanthood emerges. What does that outcome involve?

3. How is servant-humility an essential personal humble disposition in the act of Servanthood;? How is it critical for any successful leader?
4. As shown in model 3.2 model *humility, obedience,* and *willingness* is service as an interconnected overlapping relationship. What do the three characteristics of a servant share in common in the intersections HW, WO, OH, and HWO?

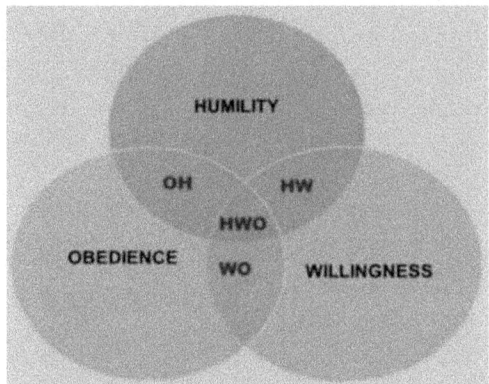

Figure 3.2 Overlapping and interconnected model Characteristics of a servant in Servanthood attribute

Practicing the Acts of the Servant-Humility

1. Jesus said: "Therefore, whoever humbles himself as this little child is the greatest in the kingdom of heaven" (Matthew 18:4, NKJV). What does the "little child" in a leader mean in this context
2. The Bible tells us; "Who is wise and understanding among you? Let him show by good conduct that his works are done in the meekness of wisdom" (James 3:13, NKJV)"Therefore, as the elect of God, holy and beloved, put on tender mercies, kindness, humility, meekness, longsuffering" (Colossians 3:12, NKJV). From these examples, how can you define personal humility?
3. How does Humility set the mind of a leader on the needs of others? Read 2 Corinthians 1-12; how did Paul demonstrate humility in this passage?
4. Setting the mind on the needs of others is to have the attitude to want to serve to please God rather than man. What two simple acts can you adopt to develop such an attitude?

CHAPTER 3
DEVELOPING THE SERVANT'S HEART IN SERVANTHOOD

5. Rate your level of humility in the acts of Servanthood attribute in Table 3.1
   (by: 1=never; 2=almost never; 3=sometimes; 4=frequently; and 5 =always) How humble are you?

Table 3.1: Level of servant-humility on Servanthood	Rate (1-5)
I see oneness, equality, and divinity all at once in others	
I perceive and see the other person's need to be served.	
I am able to get out of my mind and ego in relation to others	
I hold my own perceptions long enough to see, hear, and sense what others feel and suffer.	
I self-regulate the verbal and nonverbal behaviors in interpersonal relationships in service to others,	
I have a deep and correct self-reflection of situations others face.	
I recognize equality in others;	
I am open-minded	
I allow do not allow a sense of pride in relation to others in service and communication.	
I set my mind on the needs of others to want to serve to please God more than please man	
Total: *20/50, almost never humble* *40/50, almost always humble*	/50

CHAPTER 4
DEVELOPING A SERVANT'S HEART OF HUMILITY

Humility is at the heart of servant leadership and must be developed if a leader-servant is to be effective. Here are a few tips on how to develop the heart of humility:

Model humility by being humble

Respect your followers if you desire to be respected. Mutual respect between a leader and a follower, model's understanding and humility. Humble yourself under the hand of God and in all things and persons; admit when you make a mistake. Tell your followers how you could have done things better or explain why something was a mistake. Showing humility is part of modeling good manners and social skills; such humble attitudes and manners reflect the beauty of Christ. Tell followers why manners are important for a leader who wants to impact excellent manners in others.

Acknowledge your imperfections

How do leaders acknowledge their mistakes and imperfections in an exploitative culture, where even very well-intentioned actions can be assumed imperialism or worse? Such a culture can make leaders fear that their mistakes will be exploited, and this fear can cause them to ignore the accurate course of action at the right time. In such situations, it would be wrong to admit a mistake you did not make even though you, as the leader, are still accountable for the consequence of the mistake. A humble leader presupposes that he or she is imperfect, and readily, as a part of good leadership, honestly acknowledges his or her mistakes, knowing that only God is perfect. Here are some excellent reasons why acknowledging your mistakes develops a heart of humility:

Acknowledging your unintentional mistakes and errors demonstrates a humble heart. Unintentional mistakes and errors are innately human and are not necessarily a weakness. Some leaders find it difficult to admit they are mistaken, even when they are made aware of it. This tendency is borne out of pride; such leaders would prefer to justify and defend their mistakes in order to appear superior to seem wrong. They are quick; however, to point out others' mistakes. The ability to readily admit a mistake allows a leader to see that he or she is not infallible and can seek input from others to achieve the greater good. Such leaders see their accomplishments more as a collective effort of the people or organization. For example, Patrick Daniel, CEO of Enbridge, Inc., a North American energy and pipeline company was quoted by Jim Collins in his book, Good to Great: Why Some Companies Make the Leap...and Others Don't, as saying, "Greatness comes from humility and being at times, self-effacing." [14] Collins noted that Mr. Daniel's humble attitude was his ability to shift the focus of accomplishments away from himself and to continually recognize others' contributions. Admitting one's personal mistakes and failures is an appropriate and important mark of true humility. Admitting your own mistakes also means admitting that you are only an imperfect human. It is a sense of commitment to improve rather than making excuses. Humble leaders accept their mistakes or failures without projecting their self-worth, defending their moves, or making excuses for their failures.

Repenting to your willful mistakes develops a heart after God's own heart. An intentional mistake is a sin before God and man. They can be fatal to the trust a leader earns, especially when it is followed by deceit and manipulation to conceal. While it takes humility in a person to openly confess or admit one's sin, repentance, regret, or rendering an apology for the sin is an attitude that comes from a humble heart. Such an attitude further develops our sense of humility by helping us take a low position and listen to others so that we can heal the hurts caused by such mistakes. The attitude of repentance also helps us empathize with others, break barriers in our relationships, break our sense of pride, and destroy the ego that impedes our humility. An attitude of repentance for a mistake is a humble expression of a desire for reconciliation. It is an effective way to open the door for words of apology, such as "I was wrong," "I know I hurt you," or "I'm sorry for hurting you." For example, when David committed adultery with Bathsheba and was confronted by the prophet Nathan, David fell to the floor and wept in contrite repentance (2 Samuel 11-12). David acknowledged his intentional mistake of infidelity before God: "Wash away all my iniquity and cleanse me from my sin. For I know my transgressions, and my sin is always before me; Against you, you only, have I sinned and done what is evil in your sight" (Psalm 51:2-4). He was very remorseful, and as he expressed his repentance, he became much more humble in the process. He said; "My sacrifice, O God, is a broken spirit; a broken and contrite heart you, God, will not despise" (Psalm 51:17, NIV). God saw David as a man after His heart and allowed David to remain king until his death because he had a remorseful, repentant heart.

Enlisting the advice of others to demonstrate humility: Leaders can acknowledge their weaknesses, by enlisting the support and advice of others, even if that advice comes from a lower, unknown subject. His or her humility affords the leader a listening ear and a receptive heart. Pharaoh ruled Egypt at a critical time of hardship in the land. He demonstrated humility when he solicited the advice of others, and Joseph interpreted his dream. He was receptive to Joseph's insight and wisdom, and his humble act helped save his people from starving. (Genesis 41:1-53) This is also demonstrated in the life of Daniel and King Belshazzar. The King showed vulnerability and solicited help from others. That help came from Daniel whom there was the "spirit of excellence." Among other qualities, the King and everyone listened to Daniel because he had correct insights, a reputation of knowledge of his God, humility, and courage, and submissiveness to authority as long as God's law was obeyed (Daniel 5:23-14).

Depending on the power of God turns your weakness into strength. A leader's perception of the source of his power and control affects his ability and humility in handling his weakness. A leader who sees power as a means to get to the top or as a tool for advancing his individual strength will tend to attribute his strength to his hard work or his failures to his own weakness. However, it is God that works in us to do good works. Hence, we must depend on His power in our weaknesses

Understand God's power in weakness. In his book, Purpose Driven Life, Rick Warren discussed four actions for "God's power in your weaknesses" [15]: Admit your weaknesses, be content with your weaknesses, Glory in your weaknesses, and honestly share your weaknesses. Similar discussions are added and presented here with particular reference to developing humility in a leader-servant. Here are a few reasons why we must understand our identity and God's power in our weakness:

The richness and power of God are made perfect in our weakness. Our weaknesses reveal the richness and power of God, and acknowledging those weaknesses demonstrates humble dependence on God. A weakness is anything that makes you feeble, powerless, or helpless, and is different than a mistake. Weakness can be a symptom of a flaw in one's character such as pride, anger, or trustworthiness. Medically, weakness can be a symptom of a disease. By admitting weaknesses and vulnerabilities, great leaders demonstrate that strength for good works comes from God. Paul readily admitted his infirmities and allowed the healing and strength to come from God. Paul acknowledged that his infirmities were a "thorn" in his flesh to keep him from being conceited. It is not enough, however, to acknowledge your vulnerability and weakness. You must also have the sense that you depend on His promises. After asking the Lord to take away the thorn in his flesh, it was humbling to Paul to hear the Lord say to him, "My grace is sufficient for you, for My strength is made perfect in weakness" (2 Corinthians 12:9, NLT). This means that our weakness should make us see the power of God as an effective remedy to transform weakness into strength. In Pastor Lance Lecocq's words, "Paul asked for the thorn to be taken away, but the Lord taught him and gave him a word to deal with the sense of the presence of the thorn."

Many years ago, as a student with a large family, including four children all born over a short period of time, I was making less than minimum wage as a busboy in a restaurant and a janitor in a hotel chain. We hardly had enough money to take care of our basic needs. But I was full of faith; so rich in faith that I was called "Brother happy." All I had was faith that my heavenly Father was rich and that He would supply all my needs. And, we lived on that promise! My wife and I saw nothing in us to change our situation at the time except the strength and promises of God. Our financial woes were a weakness that revealed the richness of God as He miraculously used people we never knew or asked for help to come in strange ways to meet every need we ever had. His power brought tremendous love of people toward us. Our God was never too early and never too late, but was just on time. We know it was Him and no other and for the Glory to be His. The several testimonies of how God used those weaknesses to His glory are the subject for another book.

Acknowledging our weaknesses is very impactful in leadership. It empowers him to depend more on the Lord for strength. This allows him to humbly rejoice in those conditions for the hope of strength in Jesus. Acknowledging his weakness also reduces arrogance and feelings of superiority. It is humbling to realize that even a perfectionist can in addition make mistakes. Having the sense of imperfection reduces arrogance and the feeling of being better than others. Acknowledging one's weakness encourages an authentic relationship with followers. Most people are turned off easily by a holier-than-thou attitude from leaders whose sense of superiority causes them to talk down to others. Breaking away from such a trap creates respect and trust and so helps in building better relationships. Another impact is acknowledging one's weakness is that it increases the capacity for empathy with others. Effective empathy comes from your self-awareness of your weakness or strength. This enhances a leader's ability to heal others from self-comfort. Part of empathy is being able to project oneself into another's shoes. This is done most effectively when you can honestly share your weakness as part of encouraging and healing others.

Boasting in your sufferings is a humble surrender to God. How many of you watched the movie, The Passion of the Christ? What does the suffering of Christ mean to you? I thought I knew enough about the suffering of Christ based on what I read in the Gospel. Nevertheless, to really work through the experience through this movie was something to remember forever. During that period, I was experiencing some leadership issues with my staff. I remember saying to myself, "What a sacrifice! Why did He have to suffer like this?" To me, His suffering was an ultimate leadership born-again experience. . Paul was very dedicated to the mission of leading people to Christ. As with so many leaders who will attempt to challenge the prevailing value system, Paul was faced with persecution, hardship, and infirmities in his body. Was this the will of God for him? In addition to the infirmities being a thorn in the flesh to be humble us, Paul writes, "... We also glory in our sufferings because we know that suffering produces perseverance; perseverance, character; and character, hope." (Romans 5:2-5, NIV). Boasting or delighting in your sufferings as a humble surrender to God could be accomplished by the following actions:

Express your trust in the Lord. But does God want us to suffer? I believe that God does not want us to suffer but allows suffering in all of creation for reasons we will discuss fully later. The Bible records the story of a man named Job. "This man was blameless and upright; he feared God and shunned evil" (Job 1:1, NIV) However, God allowed Job to go through all kinds of suffering and hardship and lose all that he had through no fault of his own. Why? Job trusted God! Devil wanted to prove that the hardship would break Job such that he would curse God. God did not bring the suffering; however, It was not because of sin or Job's fault, but God did allow it (contrary to what Job's three friends assumed) to teach the lessons that even the righteous are subject to the same suffering as others. In the process of his suffering, Job's commitment to serving God despite his suffering can be seen at the level of his trust in God. He said, "Though He [God] slay me, yet I will trust Him" (Job 13:15, NKJV). His delight was in the trust he had in God!

Delight in the suffering as a path to God's providence. Job delighted in his suffering. His suffering developed in him a sense of humble repentance. They that trust the Lord will overcome suffering. Suffering is not a weakness but can cause weakness in our bodies. To suffer for the service of God is often a path we deliberately choose to take before the Lord. It is a path; we are desirous to travel or something we are willing to do despite our discomfort for the service of

God. Note that the willingness to suffer is not the same as the suffering itself. Willingness to suffer means that you willingly endure hardship, difficulty, or trials for the sake of service to God. This usually involves service to others. Delighting in our suffering is to deliberately choose a path that differs from the common one. We are not to admit our mistakes and acknowledge our vulnerabilities; instead, we are to glory in our sufferings.

Be assured that God is aware of our suffering. The Father God allowed the sinless Jesus to become the suffering of all of humanity. Though He does not want us to suffer, He allows us to go through distinctive kinds of sufferings from different sources. Some are man-made, some from illness, and some from accidents beyond our control. Others, however, are manmade, either by choice or through religious persecution. Whatever the source or type, suffering brings a variety of physical and emotional pains. "And we know that all things work together for good to them that love God, to them who are the called according to his purpose" (Romans 8:28), Job overcame his suffering and in the end, gained more than he had.

Conform your mind and surrender your will to the perfect will of God. Leaders transform their minds toward God's agenda so that they will be "able to test and approve what God's will is—his good, pleasing and flawless will" (Romans 12:2, NIV). This is important for a humble heart of service to others as exhorted by Paul: " Do not think of yourself more highly than you ought, but rather think of yourself with sober judgment, in accordance with the faith God has distributed to each of you" (Romans 12:3, NIV). The beginning of transforming a mind that surrenders to God is a humble heart with a clear-headed judgment of the unique functions and needs of each follower in the body of Christ.

Boasting only on God replaces a prideful attitude with a humble heart of thanksgiving. Pride is one of the most common reasons great men fail. It is normal for natural leaders to want a piece of glory for themselves, for their ego to be stroked a bit, or for them to stand out in the crowd for pronounced accomplishments under their leadership. The simplest path of failure in godly leaders is being too attracted to pursue the goodies of the ministry and a tendency to share the glory that belongs only to God. One key to Paul's success as a leader was that he resisted such pursuits and tendencies, and his focus was on the strength of God's wisdom and power. Paul said, "But God has chosen the foolish things of the world to put to shame the wise…to bring to nothing the things that are, that no flesh should glory in His presence. He who glories, let him glory in the Lord" (1 Corinthians 1:27-31, NKJV). Paul laid down key lessons from his own leadership experience for how leaders must respond with humility because the glory of any accomplishment belongs purely to the Lord. To give glory only to God, leaders must understand that their responsibility is to serve with humility with absolute dependency on God by taking the following four actions:

(1) **Resist the temptation** to take the glory that belongs only to God, simply focus on God's perspective and agenda.
(2) **Acknowledge your weakness**, but seek the strength of God by understanding that the power of God's wisdom can make all things possible.
(3) **Understand God's purposeful plan** in which He made the wisdom of the world foolish in order to humble the wise, to ensure "that no flesh should glory in his presence." He alone gets the glory.
(4) **Seek only God's wisdom;** "that your faith should not be in the wisdom of men but in the power of God" (1 Corinthians 2:5, NKJV)

Understanding the impact of suffering

We must understand the impact of suffering while preparing for growth. How will pain develop the strength for the growth of a great leader? Here are few reasons for boasting (glory) in our sufferings:

Sufferings produce the confident hope of a leader. A leader's assured hope makes a leader, in faith, count the suffering that he feels or sees as if it is not there. The ultimate reason for suffering is to produce confidence in the hope of the glory of God in Christ Jesus. We reach that level of hope through a process in which suffering produces the ability to persevere; indeed, perseverance develops our character, and character provides us with the foresight to sustain confident hope.

Sufferings discipline a leader to grow more spiritually. Suffering creates in us the ability to discipline ourselves to grow more spiritually with a humble heart that sees the power of God in weakness. We are to; "Rejoice always, pray continually, and give thanks in all circumstances; for this is God's will for you in Christ Jesus" (1 Thessalonians 5:16-18, NIV). The instruction is to give thanks in all circumstances; it takes absolute discipline and humility to cast all anxieties to Jesus.

Sufferings bring Christ's power upon the leader. Suffering can be a source of weakness, whether it is of our own making or outside our control. Suffering as a result of illness, loss of a loved one or loss of employment can result in hardships and an emotional situation that makes us feeble, powerless, or helpless. That is a weakness. Such weakness makes the strength of the power of God perfect. Our boasting is in the Lord for the sake of His strength and what we are in Him; spiritual leaders, in walking with God and serving others, must learn to be thankful in all situations and trust the Lord's faultless strength regardless of the circumstances.

Sufferings are the constant reminders of a leader's vulnerability and purpose in God. Devil's purpose is to frustrate the work of God by creating hardships and suffering for the leader, just as he did in the life of Job and Joseph. Suffering for the sake of our service or walk with God should only make us glad in those sufferings, because we are in his purpose and know that "All things will work together for good to those who love God, to those who are the called according to His purpose" (Romans 8:28).

Suffering produces submissive obedience. Obedience is the result of our love for God and submission to His purposeful will. Suffering can be part of God's purpose and delighting in the suffering means submitting to it. Such submission produces obedience. The author of Hebrews wrote, "And God heard his prayers because of his deep reverence for God. Even though Jesus was God's Son, he learned obedience from the things he suffered" (Hebrews 5:7-8, NLT). The true catalyst for submissive obedience is developing the heart of humility.

Suffering develops a heart of humility. Being able to take pleasure in weakness is acknowledging that our weaknesses are made perfect by the power and strength of God. We are not only to acknowledge our weaknesses; we are also to delight in them just like we are glorified in our suffering. Paul wrote, "That's why I take pleasure in my weaknesses, and in the insults, hardships, persecutions, and troubles that I suffer for Christ. For when I am weak, then I am strong" (2 Corinthians 12:10, NIV) To take pleasure in our weakness is not the same as taking pleasure for our weaknesses. Delighting in our weaknesses means to rejoicing in our weaknesses. This is a challenge for most people. How can you rejoice when you have infirmities that you are powerless to change? Or how can you rejoice in something that you have no power to control? A leader who has a sense of perfection or a superiority complex as a weakness finds it difficult or depressing to acknowledge even the slightest mistake. When leaders feel trapped in a mistake, typically against another person, the usual best response is no response at all, sometimes for fear of appearing weak. Often, the lack of being able to say, "I was wrong" can result in serious emotional hurts or expensive legal actions that could have been avoided by simply demonstrating humility. Taking delight in your weaknesses means the following to a leader-servant:

(1) **Breaking the bond of the superiority complex.** Taking delight in your weakness does not mean rejoicing in mediocrity or incompetence. It is to say, "I too have some learning to do; I have not arrived yet." It is one way a leader can break away from the trap of the superiority complex. It is to say that a prideful sense of superiority is inferiority before God as God resists the proud but gives grace to the humble. The ability to handle our sense of accomplishment without feeling superior is what makes us distinctive as leader-servants.

(2) **Showing dependence on God means delighting in your weaknesses.** A leader-servant must take delight in weakness because such an attitude allows him to not only see the strength in the power of God but also encourage the leader's faith to depend more on God. Great leaders take delight in their weaknesses because the power of God is understood much more clearly when they know their weaknesses compared to the strength of God.

(3) **Showing endurance for sacrifice means delighting in your weakness.** Enduring suffering to the point of delighting in it is an act of sacrifice. We rejoice because God is in control, even in suffering. Such an attitude gives us hope. Taking delight in weakness, suffering, or distress is one part of the attribute and sacrifice for servant leadership.

(4) **Improving relationships on all levels.** Taking delight in weakness improves relationships on all levels. As people cultivate the sense that no one is perfect, it transforms the anxiety of feeling one needs to look impeccable externally to cultivate the sense that makes God perfect in our inner strength; it encourages more honesty and openness and enhances everyone's self-confidence. A measure of humility in a great leader is in how he or she treats or values others, regardless of position or differences.

(5) **Sharing in His sufferings.** Jesus, the ultimate leader-servant, gave His life as a "ransom for many" (Mark 10:45) He suffered persecution that no other man has ever suffered. However, He humbled Himself. A leader-servant delight in his suffering to share in the fellowship of the suffering of Christ and to demonstrate his emulation of Christ's example. This is also modeled by Paul, who wrote, "Yet indeed I also count all things loss for the excellence of the knowledge of Christ Jesus my Lord, for whom I have suffered the loss of all things, and count them as rubbish, that I may gain Christ and be

found in Him...that I may know Him and the power of His resurrection, and the fellowship of His sufferings, being conformed to His death" (Philippians 3:8-10, NKJV)

Share your weakness with authenticity

Being authentic and honestly sharing your weaknesses develops your heart of humility. In Rick Warren's words, "Humility is not putting yourself down or denying your strength; rather, it is being honest about your weakness."[50] Humble leaders focus on influencing others by being authentic and by openly and honestly identifying and sharing their weaknesses rather than pretending and hiding their weaknesses to impress others. Bible says, 'God resists the proud, but gives grace to the humble" (James 4:6, NKJV. If there was ever a leader who clearly demonstrated authenticity by openly sharing his weakness; it would be the Apostle Paul. In prison, he gave hope to the free and oppressed; in his own infirmities, he encouraged those who were suffering as if there was glory in suffering. He had the strength of character to triumph over any circumstance. The Apostle Paul authentically acknowledged his own weakness in the following seven struggles in his ministry. (See Romans 7:14-24):

(1) **Sense of Entrapment:** "We know that the law is spiritual; but I am unspiritual, sold as a slave to sin" (Romans 7:14, NIV). As noted earlier, a slave is owned by the master and is under bondage to serve the master or for a master's use as he sees fit. The Apostle Paul's use of the word "as" could mean that in his "unspiritual" state, he may be a slave to sin, but he must be liberated and not remain obligated to serve sin. He devoted energy to focusing on breaking free from the bondage of habits that kept him yoked to sin.

(2) **Sense of Expediency:** "I do not understand what I do. For what I want to do I do not do, but what I hate I do" (Romans 7:15, NIV) He focused on understanding the difference between what was good to do and not expedient to do. In the words of Martin Luther King, Jr., a leader who "in fear and timidity follows a path of expediency, and social approval is a mental and spiritual slave."[51]

(3) **Sense of Inadequacy:** "For I have the desire to do what is good, but I cannot carry it out" (Romans 7:18, NIV). Paul admitted that he knew and had the desire to do the right things but fell short of carrying it out by his strength. To carry out the good works, you must focus on the power of God through the Holy Spirit by

Chapter 4
Developing a Servant's Heart of Humility

"the renewing of your mind. Then you will be able to test and approve what God's will is—His excellent, pleasing, and perfect will" (Romans 12:2, NIV)

(4) Sense of Servitude: "So I find this law at work: Although I want to do good, evil is right there with me" (Romans 7:21, NIV). The "law at work" is possibly his carnal and corrupt nature; he did not want to war in his sensuous mind; he hated to lead him against the godly dispositions he desired. This is a sense of servitude or bondage or a "yoke of slavery," that is, to do what one hates to do, "For the flesh desires what is contrary to the Spirit and the Spirit what is contrary to the flesh. They are in conflict with each other so that you are not to do whatever you want"(Galatians 5:17, NIV). To break free from this yoke, you must focus on walking by the Spirit to overcome the desires of the flesh (Galatians 5:24-25).

(5) Sense of inner struggle: "For in my inner being I delight in God's law; but I see another law at work in me, waging war against the Principle of my mind and making me a prisoner of the Principle of sin at work within me" (Romans 7:23, NIV)Focus on building your inner strength to become an inside-out leader. Servant

(6) Sense of worthlessness: "What a wretched man I am! Who will rescue me from this body that is subject to death?" (Romans 7:24, NIV). You must focus on gaining more of a Christ-likeness as a leader, as it is the only power that will deliver you from your corporeal restraints.

(7) Sense of fear. "I was with you in weakness, in fear, and much trembling" (1 Corinthians 2:3, NJKV). Nevertheless, the Apostle Paul was successful as a leader despite his fears, because he could activate his faith in God to triumph over those fears.

Depending on God develops a heart of humility

Depending on the strength that comes from God develops a heart of humility. Paul saw himself as nothing, but he accomplished much in his ministry by depending on strength from God, despite what he called "my infirmities" (2 Corinthians 12:10, NKJV) While appreciating the generosity of the Philippian Christians, Paul declared to them that his strength and sustenance were really in God. He said; "I can do all things through Christ, who strengthens me"(Philippians 4:13, NKJV). In his letter to Timothy, he said this strength comes from God, as he reminded him; "And I thank Christ Jesus our Lord, who has enabled me, because He counted me faithful, putting me into the ministry" (1 Timothy 1:12, NKJV). Paul exemplified this attitude throughout his ministry and demonstrated a strong belief that his sufficiency is indeed from the Lord, especially in his several moments of difficulties and challenges. A sense that your strength is from God, and not yourself will destroy any sense of pride and arrogance; such are the qualities that usually begin the path of failure for most leaders.

Taking Jesus' yoke demonstrates a heart of humility. Taking Jesus' yoke and learning from Him is another way we can depend on the power of God. Jesus Christ achieved much in His short ministry on earth, and yet He was very humble. Christ, in showing his humility to his disciples, modeled to them His gentleness and lowly heart and beckons them to come to him for strength through a simple act of obedience; that is taking His yoke and learning from Him. Jesus said: "Come to Me, all you who labor and are heavily laden, and I will give you rest. Take My yoke upon you and learn from Me, for I am gentle and lowly in heart, and you will find rest for your souls. For My yoke is easy, and My burden is light" (Matthew 11: 28-30, NKJV). A yoke is a long wooden beam placed between two oxen to drag them along to plow a field. It can be an emblem of bondage or domination (Deuteronomy 28:48). So, what is the meaning of Jesus saying, "Come to Me"…Take My yoke" in the context of servant leadership? Here are a few thoughts:

(1) *"Come to Me…Take My yoke"* is a no-choice command; Jesus was gently commanding leaders to come under His discipleship to learn from Him and to follow His agenda to live the life He lived; to willingly submit to authority as He submitted to His Father; Jesus was asking the disciples to relinquish their rights to be served and take up their crosses to follow Him.

(2) *"Come to Me…Take My yoke"* is the Lord's call to leader-servants to be yoked (bonded) with Him and walk alongside Him to make their burden easy. In using the word "yoke," Jesus offers a gentler kind of yoke to walk with Him with a refreshing experience rather than an oppressive, dominating one. Such dependency produces the needed relationship and humility to serve.

(3) *Leaders are to be yoked with Him* so that He can help them carry the heaviest loads to make them lighter. Jesus' yoke is easy, and His burden is light.

Our weaknesses or heavy loads are being transferred to Him at the moment we choose to be yoked with Him. When leaders are yoked with Jesus, the steps they take become His footsteps. A well-known, fictional poem, *Footprints in the Sand*, by Mary Stevenson demonstrates this principle. Quoting from this poem[17]:

One night I dreamed I was walking along the beach with the Lord. Many scenes from my life flashed across the sky. In each scene, I noticed footprints in the sand. So I said to the Lord. "You promised me, Lord, that if I followed you, you would walk with me always. However, I have noticed that during the most trying periods of my life, there has only been one set of footprints in the sand. Why, when I needed you must; you have not been there for me?" The Lord replied, "The times when you have seen only one set of footprints is when I carried you." [17]

That is the kind of mindset we need as leaders. To be Jesus' disciple, we must carry our individual cross-suffering from sorrow, defeat, sickness, or hardship- and be assured that as we follow Jesus to walk in His footsteps, He is also helping us carry the burden of the sufferings (Luke 14:27).

Cultivating a teachable spirit develops a heart of humility

A teachable spirit is a heart that is willing to learn new things and is very important in any relationship. Without a teachable spirit, we cannot grow in wisdom and knowledge. A spirit that is not teachable is always disagreeable and not peaceful. Deep down, in such a spirit is likely a feeling of superiority or a feeling that acknowledging one's weakness is a sign that one is somehow deficient. Being teachable is an essential quality of anyone who desires to grow. The lack of a docile spirit comes from an innate feeling of pride. Being teachable is also essential if one wants to be disciple or mentored, because it creates a loyal, faithful, and submissive attitude to the teacher's or mentor's authority. Here are three ways, among others, to develop a teachable spirit:

Be open-minded to learning. To be unbiased is to commit to new ideals with self-effacement that you do not have all the answers, someone knows more than you, and you can readily accept the truth regardless of the sources. Simple-minded people (open-mined people with a child-like disposition) are teachable and always growing in the knowledge of the word of God. David said, "The entrance of Your words gives light; It gives understanding to the simple" (Psalm 119:130, NJKV). Being open-minded also means that you are able and willing to learn from others, regardless of their position or diversity. The learning can be from any race, religion, socioeconomic class, and nationality that may differ from yours.

Great leaders can solicit advice from anyone without feeling inadequate. They are always learning, attending seminars, and leadership workshops to keep growing in new knowledge, updating old ideas, or learning best practices from others. They never assume that whatever competence they have is enough.

Rather, they commit to uninterrupted education and lifelong learning. This is why most professional organizations in fields such as medicine, law, accounting, and engineering require continuous education for members to update or acquire fresh knowledge regarding their profession. Great leaders learn new and better choices they can add to their talents to make them more effective and productive leaders.

A teachable spirit is a heart that is willing to learn new things and is very important in any relationship. Without a teachable spirit, we cannot grow in wisdom and knowledge. A spirit that is not teachable is always disagreeable and not peaceful. Deep down, in such a spirit is likely a feeling of superiority or a feeling that acknowledging one's weakness is a sign that one is somehow deficient. Being teachable is an essential quality of anyone who desires to grow. The lack of a docile spirit comes from an innate feeling of pride. Being teachable is also essential if one wants to be disciple or mentored because it creates a loyal, faithful and submissive attitude to the teacher's or mentor's authority. Here are three ways, among others, to develop a teachable spirit:

Be open-minded to learning. To be unbiased is to commit to new ideals with self-effacement that you do not have all the answers, someone knows more than you, and you can readily accept the truth regardless of the sources. Simple-minded people (open-minded people with a child-like disposition) are teachable and always growing in knowledge of the word of God. David said, "The entrance of Your words gives light; It gives understanding to the simple" (Psalm 119:130, NJKV). Being open-minded also means that you are able and willing to learn from others, regardless of their position or diversity. The learning can be from any race, religion, socioeconomic class, and nationality that may differ from yours.

Great leaders can solicit advice from anyone without feeling inadequate. They are always learning, attending seminars, and leadership workshops to keep growing in new knowledge, updating old ideas, or learning best practices from others. They never assume that whatever competence they have is enough. Rather, they commit to uninterrupted education and lifelong learning. This is why most professional organizations in fields such as medicine, law, accounting, and engineering require continuous education for members to update or acquire fresh knowledge regarding their profession. Great leaders learn new and better choices they can add to their talents to make them more effective and productive leaders.

Humble yourself. As humility makes one docile and so does a teachable spirit create a servant-heart that is submissive enough to want to learn. Peter's advice captures this notion: "All of you clothe yourselves with humility toward one another... Humble yourselves; therefore, under God's mighty hand, that he may lift you up in due time" (1 Peter 5:5-6, NIV). Humility is a commandment from God and not a choice for a leader-servant. We are commanded to humble ourselves before we can grow. That means that before we can add knowledge to grow in wisdom, we must be self-effacing about the need to learn. We cannot be teachable unless we are humble and able to submit to the leadership and mentoring of others. A haughty heart always disagrees with a teachable spirit. Pride has no place in a leader that wants to be great; "God opposes the proud but shows favor to the humble" (1 Peter 5:5, NIV).

Most people that focus on their reputation and achievements often see themselves as better than others. Such a mindset creates a sense of pride. Sitting in a lobby with three other deans during one of my conferences, a colleague I knew joined us at the table. In less than a few minutes, he used many words to tell us about a National Science Foundation (NSF) grant he had written and was successful because of how he wrote the proposal. In the process, he exaggerated facts He did not know that one of the deans sitting at the table served as the NSF program director for that grant and clearly remembered him and his proposal. He was humbled when this dean corrected his exaggerations. To humble ourselves is not to deny our reputation or hide it but to develop the mindset to count ourselves of no reputation. There is always someone better than you. Rather, we must focus on the reputation of the Lord or despite of others who are better than us. As Paul said, even Christ; "made Himself of no reputation" (Philippians 2:7-9, NKJV). A humble mind was in Christ when He relinquished his reputation and went to the cross or when He stooped to wash the disciples' feet.

Cultivate a listening spirit. The ability to listen is one of the desired character traits of God's followers. To develop a sense of humility, a leader must learn to hear more than he wants to speak and must constrain his tongue. The ability to listen as an attribute of a leader-servant is fully covered later in this book. To cultivate a listening spirit, leaders hunger for the truth and are in themselves secure enough to accept feedback, corrections, and constructive criticism. Moses was already a great man and a servant of God by His declaration when his father-in-law, Jethro, criticized and advised him how he alone sat in judgment all day. Moses was obviously not aware that there could be a better method of leading. Jethro, in evaluating the situation called Moses and said, "Listen now to me and I will give you some advice, and may God be with you. You must be the people's representative before God... But select capable men from all the people—and appoint them as officials over thousands...Moses listened to his father-in-law and did everything he said" (Exodus 18:19-24, NKJV)

There are times when silence is the optimum teacher and best form of listening or communication, as a demonstration that your defense is from God, and when you know that the communication is to entrap you. For example, when Christ was prosecuted, accused falsely, and sentenced to death, He chose to remain quiet. Remaining silent to hear from his inner spirit gives a leader the power to self-regulate his response. In this case, Jesus knew that it was His father's will, and what was happening to judge him to die was in line with what He already knew would take place Moses was recorded as meek and humble, but listening to Jethro was the turning point in a lesson of leadership. He learned to accept Jethro's very direct and yet constructive criticism without feeling like a failure or rejected. Moses, by his teachable spirit and humility, developed the natural intuitive leadership skills of his father-in-law.

Walking in full faith provides support for our hopes.

"Faith is the substance of things hoped for, the evidence of things not seen" (Hebrews 11:1, NKJV). Faith being the "substance of things hoped for" provides the support and the essence of our hope. Our hope in this context includes our expectations, destinations, impending life in God, final rewards, to be like Christ, eternal life, and so on The "evidence" of things not seen includes proof of the invisible things or the impossible things with man, things of the Spirit, God's presence, and His glory in our hopes, forthcoming endeavors, and so forth. What future things can a leader look for in his responsibility? What could be his possible expectations in the future?

Let us look at the case of Peter walking on water (Matthews 14:22-33). Peter, after ascertaining that it was Jesus, who was on the water coming toward them, answered Jesus' call to come. He left the boat and walked on the water toward Jesus. Peter's destination was Jesus; his hope or expectation was that he would get to Jesus. As long as his eyes were on Jesus, he remained on top of the water, evidence of the impossible things of God. When Peter took his eyes off Jesus, he saw the raging storm and began to sink only to have Jesus rescue him when he cried out for help, "Lord saves me."

What was it that caused Peter to sink? Peter started to sink not because of the impending danger of the boisterous water, but because of his doubt due to fear. Fear by nature is an innate emotional response in the face of a perceived threat or impending danger with an impulse to want to fight it or flee from it (referred to 'fight-or-flight' response). One antidote to fear is faith; the other is courage, a critical indispensable attribute of leadership. When a leader-servant takes his or her eyes off Jesus and starts to focus on the impossible or the circumstances in his or her walk, he will be wearied by the circumstances. The good news is that Peter, in his vulnerable state, remembered that Jesus was nearby. Jesus could raise him up again from the impossible situation. What other lessons can we learn about faith in walking along with Jesus in the midst of our storms? Here are four to remember:

(1) **Faith in the power of God drives the impossible.** Peter knew he was stepping onto the sea. As a former fisherman, he knew the sea very well. Yet, why did he dare to walk out on a stormy sea? It is obvious that Peter was driven by full faith in the power of God when he knew it was Jesus that called him to come. His sense of courage propelled him to answer the call, and he went with passion without minding that it was the sea onto which he was stepping. His faith dispelled any sense of fear and made the impossible walk on the water possible; he knew the sea was there, but by faith, it was as if it was not there. Walking to Jesus was his destination, and he was so concentrated on that mission that he lost focus on the stormy sea.

(2) **Fear paralyzes faith in the power of God.** A doubting faith can stop a leader from reaching his destination. Peter's initial strong sense of faith dwindled as the storm frightened him. This is very true in our lives. At the beginning of our mission, we usually see our passion and motivations rise to the highest; it is natural to see the motivation decline as the realities of the mission set in. Peter was very passionate with good intentions that he could walk to Jesus. And yet he allowed the fear of the impending danger to cause him to doubt; indeed, he sensed that the circumstance was beyond his control. Fear by nature is an innate emotional response in the face of a perceived threat with an impulse to want to fight it or flee from it (referred to as a 'fight-or-flight' response). Nelson Mandela, describing his experience in prison, said, "I learned that courage is not the absence of fear, but the triumph over it. The brave man is not he who does not feel fear, but he who conquers that fear." [53]

(3) **Faith in God resurrects the vulnerable.** Peter recognized how endangered he was but immediately remembered to cry out to the Lord. And Jesus "reached out his hand and caught him" (Matthew 14:31, NKJV) from sinking. Again, Peter's faith and passion for the walk with Jesus came to his rescue. He did not try to save himself. Rather, he knew that the Master's strength was made perfect in his weakness, and that was all he

needed. The same faith resurrected the sinking leader. Peter should be admired for being humble enough to shout for help.

(4) Faith in God silences fear. When Jesus joined the disciples in the boat, His presence alone stilled the storm and the fear of the impending danger that frightened Peter. This demonstrates the power of God and why the disciples needed to be full-of-faith leaders to silence every fear. Jesus immediately used the experience as a teachable moment when he said, "O you of little faith, why did you doubt?" (Matthew 14:31b, NKJV). In essence, He was telling the disciples that when the Lord calls them to come, you should go with loaded and active faith and not doubt. Peter started with full faith, but he then doubted. The Lord's presence stills the storms of life in a leader-servant that has the full faith to call upon Him in any circumstance without a doubt.

So, here's a great question to ponder! Was Peter a failure in this walk toward Jesus? The historical record still shows that Peter was the first and the only human to ever walk on water, even if just for a second. If his destination was to walk on water, one would say that he did not fail even though he did not finish strong. There are times a leader will face challenges that could overwhelm him as a human being and cause his faith to falter in a mission. Peter's faith faltered because of his doubt. However, one misstep or even a failed battle does not make a leader a failure in the war. Peter's destination and goal were to get to Jesus. Ultimately, Peter got to Jesus because of his faith and the other qualities of leadership he exhibited in this experience. For that, Peter reached his expected destination or his destination got to him. It is the final destination at which we arrive that will determine our success, not the first step we take or the path we follow.

A CASE OF THE POWER OF FULL FAITH IN WEAKNESS

There are many examples of my walk of faith over the years that can illustrate that the Lord will meet us at our point of need or desperation if we exercise full faith in Him. The year was 1980, and it was the last semester officially to complete my undergraduate degree program. I found out that there was a hold on my ability to enroll due to non-payment of the balance of my school fees. I was not allowed to enroll or attend any classes. As an international student, I was risking my status with the U.S. Immigration and Naturalization Service.

At the time, as Brother Faith or Brother Happy, I literally lived on the faith that my God shall supply all my needs and refused to worry or complain about my wilderness drought. Instead, I delighted in and testified to His past goodness to me. At one of these moments, I testified in Church and asked for prayers about the hold on my registration; I was convinced that God would settle my situation, but I did not know how. Out of concern and to make sure I graduated a family in church was relocating and had just sold their house. Out of their profit, they loaned me $3,000 to go pay the fees to avoid immigration problems.

Yes, it was an immediate answer to my prayer and hope in our expectations. The Lord had ministered to me days before that the bill would be paid but did not reveal how, and I was not sure if this was it.

Nevertheless, my feelings were strong that the Lord was at work in His usual way of dealing with me. I was very appreciative of this family. I had the check in my hand and was thankful that at last, I could settle the bill. Wait!!!...The greater miracle is yet to come!

On a Monday afternoon, I went to the bursar's office, which I had visited the Wednesday before. As I walked up to the counter, the same woman, I met on Wednesday waited on me.

"Excuse me, Madam, I know my fees have been paid, but could you please check?" I asked with joy and expectation.

"You were here on Wednesday," she said, "and I told you there was still a balance of about $3000. That has not changed."

"Yes Ma'am! But could you please check again"? I am convinced that the bill was paid," I insisted, still with the check in my hand. I was acting on my full faith in God's word; He desires that we, in faith, call those things that are not, as though they were (Romans 4:17)

Reluctantly, but surely, in a few minutes she came back with a reply, "I see you have a zero balance. How did that happen? Let me check with my supervisor."

She again left the counter, checked with her supervisor, and returned with a confirmation that the bill was settled late Friday last week. She was as surprised as I was overjoyed with the outcome of this Faith walk.

This and so many other miracles and encounters I experienced over the years taught me what full faith in the Lord can do for those who believe without doubting. I believed in Him and was persuaded that he would come through for me.

I returned the $3,000 check, of course, and testified how I went to the bursar's office and called the bill that was not paid as if it was, and the Lord gave me my expected hope.

I later learned that the bill was paid by my government from residual forgotten funds they were holding from my scholarship. That in itself was a Second Miracle.

The Lord is never late to a leader who trusts in Him with full faith. When Peter cried out, "Love saves me," he was rescued just as he was completing the cry. It was also full faith that propelled him to walk on the water he knew was there as if it was not. Those were Peter's assurance and expectations. You will reach your expectation to the extent you are willing to walk in full faith without doubting. It was in the act of full faith that I framed the mindset that faith is the unseen assuredness that can empower you to turn your life's probable impossibilities into great and improbable possibilities.

SUMMARY 4
DEVELOPING SERVANT'S HEART OF HUMILITY

Before starting this exercise, please read and follow the instruction in the preface of this workbook. Answers to these questions are contained in this chapter. Completion of these exercises after reading the chapter should take 60-90 minutes.

Discovering Servants Heart of Humility

1. How is humility we discovered in the earlier chapter at the heart of servant leadership?
2. Understanding the impact of suffering cultivate heart of humility
    a. How will pain develop the strength for the growth of a great leader?: (Read the section and 1 Thessalonians 5:16-18, NIV). (Romans 8:28), (Hebrews 5:7-8, NLT). (2 Corinthians 12:10, NIV)
    b. Sharing in His sufferings. A leader-servant delight in his suffering to share in the fellowship of the suffering of Christ and to

Chapter 4
Developing a Servant's Heart of Humility

    demonstrate his emulation of Christ's example (Mark 10:45). How was this modeled by Paul (Philippians 3:8-10, NKJV)

c. How can sharing your weakness with authenticity develop your heart of humility? .How did Apostle Paul demonstrate (See Romans 7:14-24) in Sense of Entrapment, Sense of Expediency, Sense of Inadequacy (Romans 12:2, NIV), Sense of Servitude: " (Galatians 5:17, NIV, Galatians 5:24-25), Sense of inner struggle. Sense of worthlessness, and Sense of fear. (1 Corinthians 2:3, NJKV).

d. How can depending on God develop a heart of humility

e. (2 Corinthians 12:10, NKJV) (Philippians 4:13, NKJV). (1 Timothy 1:12, NKJV). (Matthew 11: 28-30, NKJV).

Understanding Servant Humility Principle

1. **Understand God's power in weakness**: In his book, Purpose Driven Life, Rick Warren discussed four actions for "God's power in your weaknesses" [50]: Admit your weaknesses, be content with your weaknesses, Glory in your weaknesses, and honestly share your weaknesses. **How can such strategy help in** developing humility in a leader-servant? .

2. What are a few reasons why we must understand our identity and God's power in our weakness

3. The richness and power of God are made perfect in our weakness. What is a weakness and what does weakness do in the heart of a leader-servant? (Read 2 Corinthians 12:9, NLT).

4. What does "boasting in your sufferings" mean? Paul was faced with persecution, hardship, and infirmities in his body. Paul writes, "... We also glory in our sufferings because we know that suffering produces perseverance; perseverance, character; and character, hope." (Romans 5:2-5, NIV). How can boasting or delighting in your sufferings as a humble surrender to God be accomplished?

5. Boasting only on God replaces a prideful attitude with a humble heart of thanksgiving. The simplest path of failure in godly leaders is being too attracted to pursue the goodies of the ministry and a tendency to share the glory that belongs only to God. What lesson (1 Corinthians 1:27-31, NKJV) can you learn about how and why leaders must respond with humility?

Practicing Humility in Servant's heart

1. **A leader can model humility by being humble. How can** mutual respect between a leader and a follower model humility? How do you humble yourself under the hand of God and in all things and persons;.
2. How do leaders acknowledge their mistakes and imperfections in an exploitative culture, where even very well-intentioned actions can be assumed imperialism or worse?
3. How can you navigate a culture that create fear that acknowledging your mistakes will be exploited?
4. How can acknowledging your mistakes develop a heart of humility (Read the example of David (2 Samuel 11-12; Psalm 51:2-4; and Psalm 51:17, NIV). Why did God is these passages see David as a man after His heart.
5. **How can enlisting the advice of others demonstrate humility?.** Pharaoh ruled Egypt at a critical time of hardship in the land. How did he demonstrate humility? (Genesis 41:1-53) or demonstrated in the life of Daniel and King Belshazzar (Daniel 5:23-14).
6. **How can cultivating a teachable spirit develop a heart of humility** (Psalm 119:130, NJKV).
7. As humility makes one docile and so does a teachable spirit create a servant-heart that is submissive enough to want to learn. How does Peter's advice captures this notion?: "All of you clothe yourselves with humility toward one another... Humble yourselves; therefore, under God's mighty hand, that he may lift you up in due time" (1 Peter 5:5-6, NIV).
8. **Walking in full faith provides support for our hopes.** Let us look at the case of Peter walking on water (Matthews 14:22-33). What was it that caused Peter to sink? . What other lessons can we learn about faith in walking along with Jesus in the midst of our storms? Was Peter a failure in this walk toward Jesus?

CHAPTER 5
DEVELOPING THE ACTS OF SERVANT-WILLINGNESS

A servant's willingness to serve is a purposeful act of his inner will, eagerness, and determination to serve others without compulsion and expectation of reward or recognition. A servant willingly performs a ministry in humble obedience to the master or to meet others' needs. In this context, the Apostle Paul was proud to describe himself as a bond (slave) servant to serve others as called for by his Master Jesus; he said that he had freely given up his rights in the service of others as Jesus determined. The leader-servant's sense of willingness to commit intentionally to the service of others is motivated by his or her love for others as an extension of love for the Lord. Jesus said; "A new commandment I give you that you love one another; as I have loved you that you also love one another. By this all will know that you are My disciples, if you have a love for one another" (John 13:34-35, NKJV). This means that serving others is the natural expression that flows out of Christ's love for us. It is important to understand that the willingness to serve is not a choice but a conscious decision to submit to the commandment of God; it is obeying God to put others first.

The characteristics of willingness to serve others can be further identified from the Apostle Peter's exhortation to the believing elders: "Be shepherds of God's flock that is under your care, watching over them—not because you must, but because you are willing, as God wants you to be; not pursuing dishonest gain, but eager to serve; 3, not lordings it over those entrusted to you, but being examples to the flock. (—). All of you clothe yourselves with humility toward one another" (1 Peter 5:2-10, NIV). Willingness to serve can be demonstrated by the following:

- Purposefully putting others first;
- Setting aside self and personal agenda and serving others.
- Serving eagerly and willingly, and not grudgingly.
- Readiness to suffer for others
- Serving others without expectation of reward for us.

- Taking intentional actions and efforts to seek out and meet the need of your followers
- Involves serving with true humility, and understanding that the service is unto God as an expression of God's love and commandment to assist humbly and willingly.
- Developing Servant's Acts of Submissive–Obedience in Servanthood.

Submission is an act of love and obedience whereby one yield to the purposeful will of another. "In the same way, obedience is the act of submission where you willingly yield your will to others' will; it is a measure of a person's ability to submit to the single-minded will of another.

Understand the characteristics of submissive Obedience

Obedience as a servant has three critical characteristics to understand and develop:

Obedience is a Command: A reference to the selfless obedience to the master's command can be seen in the New Testament. Indeed, a follower of Christ or the slave of a master was designated as a servant to indicate the absolute obedience expected. A servant exercises no rights but has full commitment and submission to serving. Christ exemplified this concept when He took on the form of a servant and instructed his disciples saying, "But whoever desires to become great among you, let him be your servant. And whoever desires to be first among you, let him be your slave— just as the Son of Man did not come to be served, but to serve, and to give His life a ransom for many" (Matthew 20:26-28, NKJV). When Jesus said; "For I have given you an example, that you should do as I have done to you" (John 13:15, NKJV) He was basically giving us no choice. Instead, He gave us a command to obey.

Obedience is a call for a higher gain: Our obedience in giving up our rights in order to serve others is a call to gain something far better than what we're giving up. Jesus compared a servant's service attitude to that of a little child or "the least" among the followers. The service is unto the Lord. Hence, the leader-servant demonstrates love to God through service to others. The basis of a good leader-servant is selfless love and humility to serve others or his organization.

To followers, the leadership of a leader-servant permeates everything he does—his example and his "walking the talk," which affects the organization's missions, goals, and the well-being of others. Abraham submitted and obeyed God to sacrifice his only son Isaac, and he because the father of many nations; Moses submitted and obeyed God to lead the children of Israel out Egypt, and

Chapter 5
Developing the Acts of Servant-Willingness

God called him "my servant" Jesus submitted and obeyed the Father's will and gave up His life. He was exalted above all names under the earth.

Obedience is the fruit of submission: It is difficult to obey someone to whom you are not willing to submit. Thus, the key to generating a sense of obedience to serve is to develop a yielding spirit. A submissive spirit is one that yields to the authority or to the instruction of another person. A humble spirit and a humble spirit are two qualities that depend on each other. A modest spirit drives a leader to want to submit to learning from others, to be disciplined and corrected, and yes, to be mentored by someone else. Servant's act of submissive-obedience in Servanthood includes the following:

Follower cultivates a submissive spirit

Several relationships in the Bible showed that humility and submissiveness can be cultivated in a follower as a pathway to servant leadership. These include the relationships between Jesus and His Disciples, between Barnabas and Paul, between Paul and Timothy, Elijah and Elisha, Moses and Joshua, Naomi, and Ruth, and so many others. Let us consider the case of Moses (Leader) and Joshua (follower) and identify how cultivating a submissive spirit developed obedience in a follower like Joshua:

Followers submit to leaders' mentorship. On the eve of Moses' death, God chose Joshua to replace Moses. One of Moses' first actions was to delegate Joshua to lead the battle against the Amalekites (Exodus 17:9) in a dispute regarding water. Moses had never asked anyone to lead an attack prior to that time. Joshua respected Moses, and without hesitation, he submitted to the wish of his mentor Moses to lead the attack. He trusted Moses' judgment because he knew Moses was fully submitted to God. Joshua could have refused to submit to Moses for the fear of his own life or feeling that Moses was trying to use him. He willingly submitted even though he did not know what the outcome would be. Here are a few lessons we learned about Joshua in relation to developing a teachable spirit:

(1) **Joshua listened to instructions.** Joshua was humble enough to listen to Moses, subjecting himself to his authority and correction. He learned humility by observing Moses' sense of submission to the Almighty God.
(2) **Joshua trusted and respected Moses,** which resulted in a mentor/mentee relationship that grew into a relationship of colleagues. In the process, Joshua gained valuable leadership skills.

(3) **Joshua emulated Moses' submissiveness**. Following the example of mentors who are themselves submissive to God or legal authority is an effective way to learn to submit.

(4) **Joshua was teachable.** Good mentors develop a teachable and submissive spirit in their young leaders through their example.

(5) **Joshua walked the right path with Moses**. Moses as a mentor developed the best in Joshua by steering him in the right direction to submit to God.

The follower submits to the leader's discipleship. Joshua showed that to be a good leader, you must first be a decent follower. A humble, submissive leader readily accepts discipleship to learn more. Joshua willingly allowed Moses to disciple him. When the Lord asked Moses to come to meet Him on the mountain, he chose to go with Joshua (Exodus 24:12) and left others behind. Joshua followed and endured the 40 days and 40 nights Moses stayed on the mountain. Joshua experienced an awesome encounter with God, which was a very important and humble lesson for the young leader, who would soon walk with God. He learned the power of the God he was about to serve. Joshua submitted to Moses even when Moses changed his name from Hoshea, son of Nun, to Joshua (Numbers 13:16). There are three lessons in discipleship we can learn from Moses in his relationship with Joshua:

(1) **Leaders inspire humility in followers by modeling submission**. Moses inspired Joshua to desire to submit to walking with God. He taught Joshua how to walk with God by allowing him to watch him submit to obeying God. Then Moses released Joshua to do the work himself. Without humility, Joshua would not have emulated Moses' example, because Moses did not consult him but distinguished him from others. Joshua chose to obey by learning to submit

(2) **Leaders inspire humility in followers through reverence for authority**. Moses' reverence for God and his dedication and walk with God must have challenged and humbled Joshua as a young leader. The relationship between the two strengthened as Joshua accompanied Moses to meetings with God and as Joshua talks with Moses on their return from the mountain.

(3) **Leaders inspire humble desires in followers for independence**. Moses was fully submissive to God and the mission. Joshua wanted to learn what Moses knew. Moses instilled the desire to want to learn to become an independent, decisive leader. The result was that Moses' teaching of Joshua produced results and a legacy. In Joshua 1:8-9, we learned how submission and obedience work together. Joshua learned that walking with God means

CHAPTER 5
DEVELOPING THE ACTS OF SERVANT-WILLINGNESS

continuously meditating on the Word to obey and do all that is in the Word as commanded by God. He learned that total obedience to God's command is a condition to prosper and achieve success.

The follower submits to the leader's walk in God's presence. The more committed a leader is to learn from God and others, especially his mentors, the more clearly he sees his vulnerability and the need to cultivate a submissive spirit. For example, Moses taught Joshua to walk humbly before God. Because Joshua was very dedicated to learning, he learned quickly why the walk with God is a spiritual walk that required intimacy with God. Here are a few examples of how Joshua submitted to walk in God's presence:

(1) **Joshua submitted to a higher responsibility.** Joshua readily took advantage of Moses' mentoring to be developed into an independent leader. He submitted himself to walk along with Moses. He immediately learned that leadership carries a great sense of responsibility and understood the possible impact of his actions on the people. This was demonstrated when he was sent in the company of 11 other leaders to spy on the Promised Land (Numbers 13:16).

(2) **Joshua desired to experience God's presence.** When Moses went to have an encounter with God in the Tent of the Meeting, Joshua was in the tent with Moses and desired to experience God's presence with Moses. This young leader must have been greatly motivated to feel the presence of God and how God spoke with Moses face-face as a friend. "Inside the Tent of Meeting, the Lord would speak to Moses in person, as one speaks to a friend." Exodus 33:11

(3) **Joshua desired an independent walk in the presence of God.** He quickly learned from Moses the power of walking in the presence of God. To gain more independent experience walking with God, Joshua chose to remain behind when Moses left the Tent of Meeting to further experience the presence of God. "Afterward, Moses would return to the camp, but the young man who assisted him, Joshua, son of Nun, would remain behind in the Tent of Meeting" (Exodus 33:11, NIV). Walking in the presence of God was so important to Moses that he demanded the presence of God as a condition to continue in the exodus to the Promised Land. Moses said to God, "If your presence does not go with us, do not send us up from here... What else will distinguish me and your people from all the other people on the face of the earth?" (Exodus 33:15-16, NIV). Moses is saying here that, what distinguishes a leader-servant from others is the presence of God and

His Holy Spirit. This happens when we create a relationship and intimacy with God.

(4) **Joshua chose to have a personal relationship with God.** A leader must choose to have a close relationship with God. There is nothing as humbling and yet empowering as gaining more intimacy with God. God promised that he would never forsake us but we must commit and never forsake him learning to walk in his presence. Moses' intimacy with God was such that God would speak to him face-to-face and as a man talks to a friend (Exodus 33:11). God described his relationship with Moses as, " My servant Moses" (Joshua 1:2, NKJV) because Moses walked in God's presence. We see the same with David. He also walked in the presence of God, and God described him as a man after His heart. David said; "One thing I ask from the LORD, this only do I seek: that I may dwell in the house of the Lord all the days of my life, to gaze on the beauty of the Lord and to seek him in his temple" (Psalm 27:4, NIV).

(5) He also said to dwell in the secret place (heart of God) leaders, "must the abide under the shadow of the most high"(Psalm 91:1-3, NIV).

(6) **Joshua learned obedience and courage** as the path to victory. We learn from Joshua's report about the mission to spy on the Promised Land that if they could walk to please God, obey God, be courageous, and recognize God's protection compared to the vulnerability of the enemy without God, they would have their desired victory. Joshua said; "If the Lord is pleased with us, he will lead us into that land, a land flowing with milk and honey, and will give it to us. Only do not rebel against the Lord. And do not be afraid of the people of the land, because we will devour them. Their protection is gone, but the Lord is with us. Do not be afraid of them" (Numbers 14:8-9, NIV)

Follower submits to teachable moments to grow. Teachable moments are special times that a mentor or men-tee creates to further develop an understanding or preparation for a mission or whatever goal on which the leader desires the follower to work. Moses created several teachable moments to model and prepare Joshua for leadership. Sending him into battle, spying on the Promised Land, and meeting with God at the mountain and at the Tent of Meeting were all opportunities to teach Joshua what he needed to know about walking with God and His purposeful will. Moses knew that God would eventually direct Joshua, but Joshua at those moments needed to know how to walk with God. Here are a few examples. Creating teaching moments could mean the following:

(1) **The follower or men-tee must take the initiatives to learn independently.** Joshua also took the initiative to create independent teachable moments, such as when he remained in the Tent of Meeting to know more about God. In all these teaching moments, Joshua remained docile and humble and never questioned Moses even from the beginning when he sent him to battle. He grew to be modest and yet led as a bold and decisive leader.

(2) **The follower must find time to meditate and learn from God or a mentor.** Followers owe it to their growth to find time to relate and take advantage of growth opportunities with a mentor. God said: "You will seek me and find me when you seek me with all your heart" (Jeremiah 29:13, NIV). In David, we see a man searching for the heart of God. And David said, "My eyes stay open through the watches of the night that I may meditate on your promises" (Psalm 119:148, NIV) God rewarded David when he described him as a "man after my heart."

(3) **It is good to take time out to listen with a submissive heart.** Anyone who has waited on the Lord through prayer, and fasting knows that it can be an incredibly humbling and disciplined experience as you see yourself totally devoted to hearing from God; the more you feel like nothing before God, the further you feel closer in your walk with Him. God expects humble leaders to search for Him to indicate that they depend on Him. It means seeking Him with a heart that is fully submitted to His will.

(4) **A leader is committed to nurture and encourage followers.** The most important thing in a person's life is his or her freedom. Being totally committed to giving up his or her rights and life to nurture and encourage followers, a leader-servant inspires the growth of the community he or she serves.

To better understand this belief, one needs to understand what sacrifice means in the context of Servanthood. A sacrifice occurs when you willingly give up something important and costly to you.

Summary 5
Developing the Acts of Servant-Willingness

Before starting this exercise, please read and follow the instruction in the preface of this workbook. Answers to these questions are contained in this chapter. Completion of these exercises after reading the chapter should take 60-90 minutes

Discovering servant's willingness to serve

1. What is a servant's willingness to serve as demonstrated by Apostle Paul, or Apostle Peter (1 Peter 5:2-10, NIV) or Jesus (John 13:34-35, NKJV).
2. Willingness to serve is followed by submission as act of love and obedience whereby one yield to the purposeful will of another. How is obedience is the act of submission?

Understand the characteristics of submissive Obedience

1. What are the three critical characteristics of submissive-obedience to understand and develop?
2. When Jesus said; "For I have given you an example, that you should do as I have done to you" (John 13:15, NKJV) was it a choice or a command? How?
3. Jesus compared a servant's service attitude to that of a little child or "the least" among the followers. How does a leader-servant demonstrate love to God
4. How did the following leaders demonstrate submissive obedience?:
   a. Abraham
   b. Moses
   c. Jesus
5. Describe the servant's acts of submissive obedience in Servanthood
6. What is a submissive spirit?

Practicing acts of submissive obedience

1. How can humility and submissiveness be cultivated in a follower as a pathway to servant leadership from the following relationships in the Bible. Relationships between

Chapter 5
Developing the Acts of Servant-Willingness

    a. Jesus and His Disciples (John 15:12-14, John 9:4, 14:24) John 13:34–35;
    b. Barnabas and Paul (Acts 13, 14),
    c. Paul and Timothy (Acts 19:22, Philemon 1:1, 1Tim. 1:2; 2Tim. 1:3-5).
    d. ,Elijah and Elisha (1 Kings 19:19-21,; 2 Kings 2 and 4:38–41),
    e. Naomi and Ruth (Ruth 1:16-17),
    f. Moses (Leader) and Joshua (follower) (Exodus 17:9; Exodus 24:12; Numbers 13:16). Followers submit to leaders' mentorship. Fill in these blanks:
        i. Joshua _____ to instructions.
        ii. Joshua _____ and _____ Moses,.
        iii. Joshua _____ Moses' submissiveness.
        iv. Joshua was _____
        v. Joshua _____ the right path with Moses.
2. How do leaders inspire humility in followers?
3. How do Followers cultivate a submissive spirit?
4. How do followers submit to teachable moments to grow?.

CHAPTER 6
DEVELOPING THE ACTS OF SERVANTHOOD-SACRIFICE

A Servanthood-sacrifice is something of value, whether it is time, money, rights, position, or something else that you give up to serve others or accomplish a mission. It can also have stages, from beginning to end, and in between, depending on your commitment and urgency. Sacrifice in service leadership can be characterized by humility and people-focused intentionality in delivering service to others. Building on the humility of a servant, the sacrifice in service leadership involves the selfless love of a leader-servant that allows him to make personal sacrifices to focus on the needs of the people through intentional efforts designed to meet the growing needs of the person or the organization. One's sacrifice in service leadership of a mission has the following five core characteristics:

(1) **It is costly.** If what you give up to serve costs you nothing, it is not a sacrifice. Sacrifices have levels, from low-, moderate-, and high to extreme (ultimate) sacrifices, depending on the value you place on the assignment.
(2) **It is purposeful.** Sacrifice is specific and targeted to a purpose; it is intentionally designed to accomplish a purpose of the significance of a higher value than the cost.
(3) **It is selfless.** Sacrifice is motivated by the love to put others' rights before your rights.
(4) **It is empowering.** The level of sacrifice invested in a mission determines the outcome of the mission and inspires others to emulate the sacrifice to serve.
(5) **It is rewarding.** Although the primary purpose of a sacrifice or what one gives up is to benefit others, the service is unto God and He rewards the giver.

These five characteristics are exemplified in the example of Jesus as a leader-servant. His sacrifice cost Him. He gave "His life" (Luke 22:24-27) His sacrifice was purposeful in the sense that it served as "a ransom for many" which means it was a payment or exchange for the lives of many, condemned by sin and guilty before God. It was selfless. He did not consider His own rights. Rather, He chose not only to be a servant but also to give his life for his followers, so they could grow and be reconciled to God. It was empowering. His sacrifice empowered spiritual growth for service leadership in other people. This is very true for a leader-servant who must lead by example to empower people to follow his steps. The leader must continue to sacrifice to stay at that pyramid of leadership. And, Jesus' sacrifice was rewarding both for him and His followers. God exalted Him above all else, both in heaven and on the earth. To His followers, His sacrifice brought salvation and reconciliation of man to God.

An important sacrifice for a leader-servant is the willingness to share power and control. Power control is a critical, dominant element of any secular leadership philosophy and runs contrary to servant leadership. It is generally the most difficult thing for leaders to relinquish, and yet it is one of the most effective ways to empower growth when handled purposefully. For example, the all-powerful Holy God suffered for powerless, sinful mankind. He adopted us as brethren, even though He created us all, and shared our humanity, even though he was the perfect savior. This was all for empowering reconciliation in us (Hebrews 9:12). At the peak of the pyramid of His sacrifice, He emptied Himself of every right on the account for all that He was called to do. A leader-servant gives up his rights and assumes that no sacrifice is too much for the growth of his followers. Other sacrifices that Leader-servants can make include (but are not limited to) those listed in Table 10.

Table 10: Personal rights and privileges

Personal rights and privileges	
Pride	Popularity
Desires	Familiar surroundings

CHAPTER 6
DEVELOPING THE ACTS OF SERVANTHOOD-SACRIFICE

Control	Status
Freedom	Dignity
Comfort	Time
Independence	Possessions
Impatience	Humanity
Power	Authority
Life	Position
Self	Resources
Will	Recognition
Agenda	Interest

What rights have you given up or what sacrifices are you willing to make to serve others? Paul, as a fellow human, also gave up his rights to be all things to all men (1 Corinthians 9:5-15). To give up something in this context does not mean that you do not own those things or have those rights. It means that other things about your service and purpose in God take a higher priority over your rights. This is at the heart of Servanthood—relinquishing the right to be selfish. Leaders increasingly gain a servant's heart by denying "self" to please and develop others by adding value to their lives. A leader, who can accept mistreatment and readily forgive wrongs, imitates Christ as a model.

THE SEVEN LEVELS OF ULTIMATE SACRIFICES

An ultimate sacrifice in His service to reconcile us to God is shown in Jesus' example as identified by the Apostle Paul: "In your relationships with one another, have the same mindset as Christ Jesus: Who, being in very nature God, did not consider equality with God something to be used to his advantage; rather, he made himself nothing by taking the very nature of a servant, being made in human likeness. And being found in appearance as a man, he humbled himself by becoming obedient to death—even death on a cross!" (Philippians 2:5-11, NKJV)

Below are the seven levels of sacrifices and what Jesus gave up to relationally reconcile humanity to God:

1. **His Identity. He gave up His divine form. This** is very significant when evaluated in terms of cost. His divine form was what made Him God and unique and very high in his act of service.
2. **His Authority.** He gave up his status and positional authority. Once He was willing to give up His divine form, it was easy to empty Himself of the rights of His divinity. This does not mean that He did not have those rights. He was still God but chose to set the work of salvation to a higher priority to God the Father and set those rights aside. He made himself lower than angels, even though angels worshiped Him.
3. **His Immortality.** He gave up His immortality. Giving up his identity, his self-sufficiency, and all divine rights, He was willing to bring Himself down to the level of mortal man. The immortal God exchanged His immortality for mortality so as to make Himself visible to man.
4. **His Control.** He gave up His freedom to be in control. As a man at humanity's level, He emptied Himself of any rights that a man has, His freedom, His control, and His status to become a servant, a slave to the call. The loss of His freedom and control made Him less than a liberated man. He became a slave and gave His body to be tortured.
5. **His Power.** He gave up His power and control. He had control of His life, but He chose to relinquish it and allowed Himself to be betrayed and sentenced to die. He knew He was being betrayed, and He could have stopped it; nevertheless, He chose to submit to the Father's will and accepted the obvious and manipulations.
6. **His Life.** He gave up His life. He not only was agreeable to become a servant, but he was also consenting to be lower than a servant who was willing to give up his right to

life by being obedient. The self-sufficient and omnipotent God gave all up to serve the purpose of God for the love of humanity.

7. **His Dignity.** He gave up His self-worth. Finally, he not only died, but he died the worst kind of death; indeed, lower than death itself, he suffered humiliation and death on the cross. (Curse is a person that dies on the cross.) He exchanged and tasted death for sinners, even though He was the sinless, immortal God, who had power over death.

Again, we see that these sacrifices were priceless they cost Him His own life; they were purposeful in reconciling humanity to God; they were selfless and humanity-centered and not for Him to be served. It was about the salvation of humanity. The sacrifices were also empowering because His death and strength to overcome were made perfect humanity's weakness. For these sacrifices, He furthermore, received the ultimate reward, for God exalted Him above all names; in His name, all knees shall bow and all tongues shall confess that Jesus is Lord.

DEVELOPING THE ACTS OF SACRIFICE-SELFLESSNESS

Selflessness means the readiness to give up self (personal concerns, desires, and needs) and focus more on others' needs without expectation of reward. It means that a leader-servant must be other-centered and not self-centered in his or her approach to service. Paul, writing to the Christians in Rome said, "We then who are strong ought to bear with the scruples of the weak, and not to please ourselves. Let each of us please his neighbor for his good, leading to edification. For even Christ did not please Himself" (Romans 15:1-3, NKJV). Jesus Christ, who was 100% God and 100% man "made himself nothing" (Philippians 2:7). How can leaders be selfless in these days where most leaders in this capitalistic age seek for their own self-interest? The characteristics of selflessness of a servant in

Servanthood can be identified as others-centeredness, love of humanity, and intentionality as demonstrated below:

Be others-centered:

Others-Centered service in the servant leadership model is intentional and motivated by the selfless love of others. Leaders seek to transform an organization by developing the service mindset of followers; the leader pushes for the rights of others more than his rights and inspires them to grow to follow the leader's example, as Jesus demonstrated: "...But whoever desires to become great among you, let him be your servant. And whoever desires to be first among you, let him be your slave". (Matthew 20:26-28, NKJV). Being others-centered also means that our success as leaders comes through sacrifices and self-denial for the service and well-being of others.

Be contented in God's things

As God said to the Prophet Jeremiah; "Do you seek great things for yourself? Do not seek them!"(Jeremiah 45:5); instead, find contentment and satisfaction in the work God has given to you. Do things heartily unto God and not men (Colossians 3:23)? Be an example of uprightness in all circumstances, "Teaching us that, denying ungodliness and worldly lusts, we should live soberly, righteously, and godly, in this present world" (Titus 2:12, KJV). Being centered in God's things also means having no fellowship with the unfruitful works outside of God.

Let the love of humanity be your motivator.

Love of followers is both the starting and ending points of service leadership. First, God's love of mankind was the attribute that defined the work of salvation and His reconciliation of mankind to Himself (John 3.16). Peter demonstrated how we can show love in our attitude of service to each other (1 Peter 3: 8-13). We are to be of one mind and unified in purpose just as Jesus, and the Father; the Almighty God are unified in purpose; we are to be compassionate with one another as one way of bearing and empathizing with one another and showing practical love to each other; we are also to be

Chapter 6
Developing the Acts of Servanthood-Sacrifice

tender-hearted; this allows us to readily forgive each other and repay evil with blessings. These positive attitudes are direct manifestations of the fruit of the Spirit and a measure of the quality of the spiritual work of a leader toward others. Paul wrote; "But the fruit of the Spirit is love, joy, peace, forbearance, kindness, goodness, faithfulness, gentleness and self-control. Since we live by the Spirit, let us keep in step with the Spirit. Let us not become conceited, provoking, and envying each other (Galatians 5:22-26, NKJV). This means that the Spirit of God in a leader should yield the fruits of the Spirit. This, in turn, should produce fruit and affect the people served. A leader can only produce in others the identical fruit he has inside and can display outwardly. In other words, how the measure of how much love, joy, and peace your work brings, is how much of the same you can demonstrate to others. Are you happy with your work? Do people around you feel loved and joyful? How forbearing and kind are you when you serve others? What level of goodness and faithfulness does your work show to others? In rendering your service, how much gentleness and self-control do you show?

Your love of others is defined by what your acts of love do. How are you doing in each of the attributes of love delineated in II Corinthians 13? Love of humanity is at the core of what drives our work as leaders. I stated a Law of Conservation of God's Love: *God's Love is Conserved Even in Our Sufferings.*[19] God is LOVE; His love is CONSERVED, that is, does not change but can be transformed, and His Love is perfect in our SUFFERING. These are some of the most critical elements of God's love for humanity and set the standard for our selfless love and disposition toward others. Love is characterized or known to us by the things it does (1 Corinthians 13:4,8, NKJV):

(1) God's Love is Divine, characterized by other-centered actions: Patience (long-suffering toward others), Kindness (the tendency to be sympathetic and compassionate, and caring toward others), Generosity (willingness to freely give toward the need of others), Humility (not prideful toward others), Courtesy (respectful to others), Unselfishness (putting the general good or the needs or interests of others first), Good

Temper (never resentful toward others), Godliness (thinks no evil and is gladdened by goodness to others), Truthfulness (an act of telling the truth), Forgiveness (bears all things, pardoning others for a mistake, wrongdoing, offenses), Trustworthiness (the capacity to trust others or be trusted by the same), Long-suffering (being patient or tolerant toward others);

(2) God's Love is conserved and never changes. There is no fear in suffering, for He will take the hardship and bring good out of it. This means that suffering is transformed into good within God's purposeful will. And

(3) God's Love is perfected in suffering. In the mix of suffering, we must remain undaunted and have the mind to delight in the suffering for His sake.

DEVELOPING THE ACTS OF COMMITMENT IN SACRIFICE

The personal and purposeful commitment to the growth of others is borne out of the motivation to want to serve others for the specific purpose of the others' growth; it is mainly driven by the intuitive conviction on the purpose of the service to others. The level of individual commitment to serve others is based on an intimate sense of values and core beliefs that drive a leader's intentionality in his act of service.

The personal commitment is purposeful to the level to which the service is mission-focused. Great leaders are focused on the mission based on their value system and understanding of God's perfect will. Commitment gives the leader a convincing intention for the decision to make about the work. Commitment sustains the leader's focus on the service and leads to intentional action and decisiveness as characteristics. Decisiveness is the external action of a leader's internal ignition to act; it is driven by a sense of discernment and instinctive conviction on the purpose of the service. In discerning, the leader must be an excellent Influencer, intuitive, flexible, and have a good sense of conviction and decisiveness to act when necessary.

Summary 6
Developing The Acts of Sacrifice in Servanthood

Before starting this exercise, please read and follow the instruction in the preface of this workbook. Answers to these questions are contained in this chapter. Completion of these exercises after reading the chapter should take 60-90 minutes.

Discovering Servanthood-sacrifice Attribute

1. Define a Servanthood-sacrifice
2. What are the five characteristics of sacrifice in service leadership?
3. How are these five characteristics exemplified in the example of Jesus as a leader-servant.
4. What are willing to sacrifice in leadership? And what can you not sacrifice?

Understanding the Principle of Servanthood-Sacrifice

1. An important sacrifice for a leader-servant is the willingness to share power and control. How can sharing power be the most effective way to empower growth? (See Hebrews 9:12).
2. How do you define your love of others? How are you doing in each of the attributes of love delineated in II Corinthians 13? Love of humanity is at the core of what drives our work as leaders.
3. Love is characterized or known to us by the things it does (1 Corinthians 13:4,8, NKJV). What is the foundation of these qualities of love?
4. State the Law of Conservation of God's Love: how does the critical elements of God's love for humanity set the standard for our selfless love and disposition toward others?
5. How is God's Love characterized by other-centered actions?
6. What are three characteristics of selflessness of a servant in Servanthood Read also (Romans 15:1-3; Philippians 2:7).

7. What does is mean to be others-centered in service? : (Matthew 20:26-28, NKJV).

Practicing Acts of Sacrifice in Servanthood

1. Why is Power control in practice the most difficult thing for leaders to relinquish?
2. Paul, as a fellow human, also gave up his rights to be all things to all men (1 Corinthians 9:5-15). What rights have you given up or what sacrifices are you willing to make to serve others?
3. In table 6.2, below rate you ability to make the following sacrifices
   (by 1 = never; 2 = almost never; 3 = sometimes; 4= frequently; and 5 =always)

Personal rights and privileges			
Sacrifice	**Scale 1-5**	**Sacrifice**	**Scale 1-5**
Pride		Popularity	
Desires		Surroundings	
Control		Status	
Freedom		Dignity	
Comfort		Time	
Independence		Possessions	
Impatience		Humanity	
Power		Authority	
Life		Position	
Self		Resources	
Will		Recognition	
Agenda		Interest	

4. What does to give up something in this context of leadership mean?

CHAPTER 6
DEVELOPING THE ACTS OF SERVANTHOOD-SACRIFICE

5. How can relinquishing the right increase your gain as a leader-servant?
6. How did Jesus demonstrate the Seven Levels of Ultimate Sacrifices (Philippians 2:5-11, NKJV) to relationally reconcile humanity to God:
   a) His Identity.
   b) His Authority.
   c) His Immortality.
   d) His Control.
   e) His Power.
   f) His Life.
   g) His Dignity.
7. What does selflessness mean in the context of service? How do you develop the Acts of Sacrifice-Selflessness?
8. How is being contented in God's things a quality of selflessness? (see Colossians 3:23)? world" (Titus 2:12, KJV).
9. How is the love of followers the starting and ending points of selfless service leadership?
10. The personal and purposeful commitment to the growth of others are borne out of the motivation to want to serve others for the specific purpose of the others' growth. What is the role of personal commitment in acts of servanthood-sacrifice in other-centered service?

CHAPTER 7
DEVELOPING THE ACTS OF INTENTIONALITY

Intentionality for growth is a selfless deliberate act of a leader motivated by the love to serve others by purposefully creating growth opportunities. As an element of a servant's selflessness in the act of Servanthood, intentionality presupposes a commitment to others-centeredness and love of others. Jesus, without coercion, intentionally "made Himself" of no repute so that others can be reconciled to God. He "emptied Himself" (of His glory and eternal riches, independence, power, divinity, dignity, and life) and came down to the level of man so that man can go up in relational level with God (Philippians 2:7). Intentional efforts are designed to meet the growing needs of others. The three primary pathways for growth intentionality are sharing power to inspire growth, a personal and purposeful commitment to the growth of others, and a willingness to serve.

Sharing power to inspire growth

Sharing power to inspire growth in others is a biblical concept. Paul acknowledged the impact of his partnership with the Philippian believers (Philippians 1:5) and with Timothy on the common goal for the spiritual growth of believers: "For as we share abundantly in Christ's sufferings, so through Christ, we share abundantly in comfort too" (2 Corinthians 1:5). To Paul, we are one in the ministry together as a team with Jesus Christ as the leader: "For we are God's fellow workers. You are God's field, God's building" (1 Corinthians 3:9, ESV). A selfless follower-centered Leader–Servant has a sense of accountability for the spiritual growth of his followers. He can intentionally inspire growth in his followers by the following key strategies fully discussed in The Leader as Servant Leadership Model: [19]

Share and communicate the vision to inspire growth. A leader's vision for the growth of followers specifies in the present what each follower's growth should be in the future. The vision defines the growth opportunities to be created; the vision is clear and purposeful when it provides focus, meaning, and values the leader's mission for the growth of the followers. For example, "in three and half years, each disciple will experience an abundant Christ-like life of service to each other," could be a vision statement of Jesus' mission on earth for His leadership of the disciples. The leader's important step after articulating his vision is to empower others to share in the vision by showing them how they can achieve more fulfilled growth that bears much fruit. Nehemiah shared the vision of how rebuilding the broken walls of Jerusalem would remove the reproach on Israel.

Share critical information to empower growth. We've often heard that "information is power," thus sharing information means sharing power. Sharing information with followers and soliciting their input in important decisions that will impact their lives increases the followers' sense of meaningfulness. This provides open channels of communication and direct engagement in decision-making. It also communicates that the organization values its members. In a competitive, fast-paced environment, quick reactions to rapidly dynamic market conditions can cause a change in the company's performance. Being part of the change helped each member commit personally to absorbing the impact of the change. It was an act of transparency that built mutual trust between the followers and the leader.

Share power and control to relinquish or delegate some leadership rights, power, and responsibilities to others. A selfless Leader–Servant sees power and control as an end to the means, with the growth of followers being the means. Rather than controlling followers, Leader–Servants empower followers to grow. Sharing power insures that all members of an organization feel included, valued, and engaged in building good relationships and a thriving community. When power is shared, members of the organization feel respected, powerful, and appreciated in their position in the relation to the organization.

Chapter 7
Developing the Acts of Intentionality

Share common purpose and action for performance. This process begins with defining and communicating shared values, engaging people in beneficial actions based on joint values, and helping to develop the confidence to accept high challenges and responsibilities. There is a direct, favorable correlation between the way people perceive their organization and engagement in the organization, and performance. A positive organizational culture that allows leaders to share power can significantly escalate followers' performance through increased enthusiasm, motivation, and confidence.

Share yourself to connect with and empower others. This is done by sharing yourself honestly (failures and successes) to connect with your followers. Your followers do not often understand the road you have walked and the challenges you have faced to get where you are in the leadership pyramid. Authentically sharing your personal stories to connect in relation to the followers' challenges is very impacting. In my years as an academic professor, one of the most effective ways, I have empowered students to move toward excellence was by being authentic and sharing my experiences. And I do have a lot of them—both good and bad, successes and failures. The following strategies can be used as a process in sharing yourself with others you are mentoring:

(1) **Emphatically listen to their stories** or situations to understand them. It is critical to listen to them carefully, attentively, and reflectively on the content of what they are communicating. Your attention communicates s that you care and first sign of your empathy toward them.

(2) **Identify the success you can affirm in** them before the failures. Because the goal is to empower the follower for excellence, and to meet a sought-after performance goal; it is important to identify success carefully, specifically some intangibles. Encourage and empower them with words of affirmation to give them hope and confidence; words that express the value of their success to their desired goals; words to give them a picture of success and what that could mean if they progressively multiple successes to other areas.

(3) **In identifying specific challenges or failures.** First, focus on identifying the attitudinal failures of the follower, which they communicate directly. Attitudinal failures include such things as, "I forgot…", "I was late…", and "I did not pay close attention."

Second, we (leaders with followers' involvement) identify retention failures. These failures occur due to poor mastery of the subject or concept, which results in a lack of understanding and an inability to retain and use concepts. Third, we identify the reckless failures and why they were made. Careless failures include lazy or sloppy errors that students or followers can make on things they know and should get right. These are usually the most painful mistakes and these can cause them to feel like failures.

(4) **To admonish followers on these failures.** It is most effective from the start to mutually agree or identify the characteristics of "an intelligent follower." A bright follower is accountable for his or her focus, motivation, and perseverance for his success regardless of the challenges or barriers presented. In general, admonishment is an important part of discipleship and empowering followers. This is done effectively through precise affirmations, as well as cautionary words of rebuke designed specifically for correction.

Make others' growth a personal mission

It is important to give followers the self-confidence that allows them to achieve more by helping them see how correcting some of the errors or failures is within their control. This is effectively done by mutually understanding and developing what I have defined as an Intelligent Follower.[19] The three characteristics of an Intelligent Follower and the process for inspiring growth are defined as follows:

(1) Self-awareness and knowledge of personal weaknesses, needs, and assets. This requires the follower to be self-aware of what he does not know, what he knows, and the empowering actions (referred to as growth-enabler), to fill the competency gap.

(2) Motivation and self-will to want to know what he does not know. This requires self-motivation and self-will to use his growth enabler to fill the knowledge gap; he must diligently and readily seek help and resources to fill his identified competency gap; procrastination only widens the knowledge gap and must be avoided at all costs.

(3) Resilience and perseverance to apply what he knows to advance. The follower must apply what he knows, his small successes, and his identified assets to advance in his growth beyond the knowledge

CHAPTER 7
DEVELOPING THE ACTS OF INTENTIONALITY

gap. This third characteristic is what develops the follower into a leader. It is what increases the retention and application of knowledge. In my many years of applying this model to mentoring students, it transforms a B- grade into an A-grade student or failure due to a lack of focus on success. This is a different kind of intelligence. It is what I will refer to as SMART Intelligence- the ability to adopt strategic, measurable, achievable, reasonable, and tractable means to train for and acquire new knowledge. The process is summarized in Table 7.1.

(4) The model can also be applied to develop great organizations to turn their weaknesses into incredible successes. The process starts by taking control of your growth and identifying your strengths and weakness in relation to your personal growth, working on your growth opportunities.

Table 7.1: Personal development of Intelligent Follower [54]

Characteristics of Intelligent Follower	Strategies for developing self-leadership for follower's personal growth
Self-awareness of knowledge gap- weakness, needs, and assets: • Identify what you do not know • Identify what you know • Mark the *knowledge gap*	Identify the things you currently lack, specific set of competency skills, experience, resources you know will help your growth but you lack them
	Identify your challenges, limitations, small past success or experiences; Identify challenges you anticipate in meeting those needs
	Identify your important strategic assets (resources, interests, strengths, experiences). These are the *growth enablers*
Motivation and self-will to want to know what is not known:	Identify strategies you are willing and able to follow and those you are willing but unable to follow and reason why Examples: Bible study, more training, homework help, peer-mentoring

• Use the growth enablers to know • Diligently seek help and resources to fill the knowledge gap above	Diligently use the growth enabler—resources available – to meet challenges to fill your immediate growth and knowledge gaps
	Example: good study habits, teachable spirit, teachers, talents you know you have.
	Align your key action to each of the lacks above, focusing time and limited resources on the priorities that matter most
Resilience and perseverance to apply what you know to advance: • Application of smaller successes; • Use identified assets to advance beyond the knowledge gap.	Persevere to diligently apply what you know to practice for spiritual and professional growth; Apply growth opportunities to your personal success
	Apply the small successes you can focus on to persevere beyond your current need
	Get the reason of any perceived failure and resilient to use those for increased success

SUMMARY 7
DEVELOPING THE ACTS OF INTENTIONALITY

Before starting this exercise, please read and follow the instruction in the preface of this workbook. Answers to these questions are contained in this chapter. Completion of these exercises after reading the chapter should take 60-90 minutes.

Discovering Acts of Intentionality

1. What is intentionality in the growth of others? What role does intentionality play in servant's selflessness in the act of Servanthood (See Philippians 2:7).
2. What are three primary pathways for growth through intentionality?

CHAPTER 7
DEVELOPING THE ACTS OF INTENTIONALITY

3. How did Apostle Paul demonstrate intentionality by sharing power to inspire growth? (See Philippians 1:5; 2 Corinthians 1:5; 1 Corinthians 3:9).
4. A selfless Leader–Servant sees power and control as an end to the means, with the growth of followers being the means.. What happened to members of the organization when power is shared? ; what happens to the organization at the same time?

Practicing the acts of Intentionality

1. The process of sharing common purpose and action for performance begins with defining and communicating shared values, engaging people in beneficial actions based on joint values, and helping to develop the confidence to accept high challenges and responsibilities. What is the correlation between the way people perceive their organization and engagement in the organization to their level of performance in the organization?
2. First step in the practice of intentionality is to make others' growth a personal mission. How can this be done to increase followers' performance?
3. What are the three characteristics of an Intelligent Follower and the process for inspiring growth?
4. What is "SMART Intelligence"? How can you initiate SMART Intelligent in a follower?

CHAPTER 8
DEVELOPING THE ACTS OF SERVANTHOOD-SERVICE

Service leadership focuses on the leader's engagement and empowerment of followers for maximum productivity or fruitfulness in service to others. Our expression and willingness to serve are very important, but if the process of delivering that service or serving is not clearly defined, it will affect the quality of the duty of the Service leadership which is one of the four dimensions of the Leader as the Servant Leadership fully discussed in the book. The Servanthood attribute is effective to the extent that the leader has a positive attitude toward the service. The service attitude is the primary approach a leader takes in service to others. Such a positive other-centered approach creates and sustains the interconnecting relationships required to understand and meet the needs of those being served. Service in Servanthood is characterized by people-centeredness in service, focus on good works, a sense of purpose for the service, and passion for the service.

People-centered service in Servanthood.

For a leader- a servant to be people-centered in Servanthood, he must have appropriate people's skill characteristics such as:

(1) *Awareness of self and followers;* this includes self-cultural awareness and a deep understanding and control of one's own biases;
(2) *Intercultural competency skills,* including the ability to develop a positive attitude toward interacting and communicating with people with backgrounds, perspectives, or cultural values that differ from yours;
(3) *An Authentic relationship is based on a genuine love for humanity;* a legitimate relationship is a state of connectedness or relatedness between people (especially an emotional connection). Over time, such a relationship will create trust and confidence.

Some key points can be made about why the love of humanity is an essential driver for a leader's service that is centered on people:

a). Jesus' love of mankind was the attribute that defined God's work of salvation (John 3:16). The completed work of salvation and love for mankind was so important to God that He allowed the sinless Christ to die to reconcile sinful man to Him. David said; "Since they show no regard for the works of the Lord and what his hands have done, he will tear them down and never build them up again" (Psalm 28:5) God's purpose must be accomplished despite us. So, a leader must be ready to serve to complete the work God has called him to do.

b). Peter illustrates an example of how we can show the attitude of service by being other's focused (1 Peter 3: 8-13):

Be of one mind and unified in purpose. Jesus showed the love he shared with the Father by demonstrating unity between Him and the Father. He expects such unity to exist between believers, especially in the service of God. He taught against a divided house, and Peter and Paul followed the same example.

Be compassionate with one another. The ultimate result of our Servanthood is the affection and kindness we show to each other. This comes from compassionate, tender hearts that are able to empathize with each other.

Be humble. Humility is the first driver for a heart that wants to serve others. Humility is the motivator that allows you to see others at the same level or allows you to put others ahead of yourself.

Focus on good works in the Servanthood service

Our work must be evaluated constantly to assess our progress in meeting intended goals. The following self-assessment questions can be used to measure "good" works in service:

(1) **Faith test:** Does the work arise out of your active faith and living out the life of Christ in you?

(2) **Glory (Pride) test:** Does the work bring glory to God or to you? Evaluate the primary purpose of what we do in service to others and for God to receive the glory.

(3) **Impact test:** Does our work impact others? Your work must yield Christ-like fruit that impacts people around you. A direct measure of our good works is the growth of followers.

(4) **Conformity test:** Is the work being done in conformity with the written word of God? Good work results from our acts of love and our method of carrying out the work.

Chapter 8
Developing the Acts of Servanthood-Service

(5) **Consistency test:** Does the work align with a walk with God? Good works result from the leader's consistent walk with God in three critical acts of service:
   a) Work with a purpose for the service,
   b) Work with passion for the service, and
   c) Work with perseverance for the service.

Sense of purpose of the service

A positive sense of purpose in the service is an essential element for the service that pleases God and not man. Such a mindset helps to cultivate humility in our acts as Servanthood; great leaders, who see a purpose to be bigger than they can envision, see no reason to be proud or blow their trumpets. There are enough people around them to do that, even for a greater honor. Rather, they act as servants and do not allow what they are or have done to distract them from God's agenda. According to the Apostle Paul, we leave such things behind and press on to win the prize of our higher calling in God. Leaders such as Paul see themselves as too small in the eyes of what God is so that they always retain the glory for Him. Focusing on God rather than ourselves shows we understand the purpose of our calling. To develop humility and avoid "eye service" where you want others to notice you and praise you, Paul, in writing to the Galatians asked; "For do I now persuade men, or God? Or do I seek to please men? For if I still pleased men, I would not be a bondservant of Christ" (Galatians 1:10, NKJV)

Basically, the leader's focus to cultivate humility is to have a sense of Servanthood (bondservant) toward service and do all he can to please God. Jesus also said; "Take heed that you do not do your charitable deeds before men, to be seen by them. Otherwise, you have no reward from your Father in heaven" (Matthew 6:1). To take heed is to pay attention that the intents of our hearts are not to please men.

Developing passion for the service

Passion for service in Servanthood is an essential element for a leader to be conditioned for service leadership. Passion for the service can be characterized by a passion to serve others, a mind to suffer to sustain the passion, and a desire to walk with followers and God with passion:

Be passionate about service to others. The passion of a leader-servant for the work creates the desire to understand the purpose of the work. Paul said; "For though I am free from all men, I have made myself a servant to all, that I might win the more…I have become all things to all men that I might, by all means, save some. Now, this I do for the gospel's sake, that I may be partaker of it with you…" (1 Corinthians 9:19-27). From these scriptures, we learn the following results of Paul's passion:

(1) *Passion to serve all men.* Paul's passion was to serve all men, and he could discipline himself to become adaptable to serve all men in all circumstances.
(2) *Passion to be slaves for all men.* He was "free from all men" and yet passionate as a slave for all men to gain more for the mission.
(3) *Passion to reach all people.* Paul set aside his personal preferences and rights to reach all people he needed to reach with the gospel.
(4) *Passion to fulfill his mission.* His passion drove his selfless desire to fulfill his mission to win those that were without the law.
(5) *Passion to become all things to all men.* Paul knew and understood what was worth dying for and valued the people he was called to serve and so was passionate enough to become all things to all men.
(6) *Passion for a disciplined focus.* Paul's passion also created in him a strong sense of discipline that kept him focused on the mission and flexible in the method he used. "For consider Him who endured such hostility from sinners against Himself, lest you become weary and discouraged in your souls" (Hebrews 12:3).

God's purpose in a leader's life may take the leader out of his comfort zone. We see missionaries who, after being called to difficult areas of service, often share their challenges and fears in the field of work.

Have a mind to suffer to sustain the passion. The second desire for understanding the purpose of work is to have a mind to suffer in order to sustain passion. As noted, suffering is a path that a leader-servant is willing to take for the sake of serving God. The concept of "a mind to suffer" is a deliberate willingness to choose or endure a path outside our comfort zone. Passion for work means that we must have the mind to suffer. Simon Peter, in writing to encourage believers who were frightened by the persecution of the Roman Empire, saw suffering as a path to remaining passionate about the purpose of their lives. Nothing good comes easily.. Great men do not get their height in a sudden flight. Peter wrote, "Therefore since Christ suffered for us in the flesh, arm yourselves also with the same mind, for he who has suffered in the flesh has ceased from sin" (1 Peter 4:1, NKJV). Peter made it clear that suffering is part of a leader's purpose in the work of God and is a direct act of emulating Christ, who suffered it all, even death at the cross. He reassured frightened believers when he said;

Chapter 8
Developing the Acts of Servanthood-Service

"For to this you were called, because Christ also suffered for us, leaving us an example, that you should follow His steps" (1 Peter 2:19-25, NKJV).

A leader-servant must arm him- or herself with this basic character. Your willingness to suffer is not the same as experiencing the hardship itself. Rather, it means that before God, you choose to endure hardships, trials, and difficulties as exemplified in the life of Jesus and the Apostle Paul in their examples of humility and suffering. Paul said; "We consistently carry around in our body the death of Jesus, so that the life of Jesus may also be revealed in our body. For we who live are always delivered to death for Jesus' sake, that the life of Jesus also may be manifested in our mortal flesh" (2 Corinthians 4:10-12, NIV).

Great leaders are not frightened by suffering. In Peter's words; "But in your hearts, revere Christ as Lord. Always be prepared to answer everyone who asks you to give the reason for the hope that you have" (1 Peter 3:15, NIV). Below are several key strategies to cultivate the mind to suffer to sustain the passion for the purposeful work of God:

(1) **Take suffering as part of the purpose for life.** We must take suffering as unto God and hold Him dear to our hearts. By doing so, we can remain passionate about the work when there is suffering involved in our mission.
(2) **Cultivate readiness to give an account of your hope in the mission.** We must be ready to give the account of the hope in us with humility and respect. This happens only if we understand the purpose of the work.
(3) **Cultivate a sense of willingness to suffer.** Cultivate a sense of willingness to yield to the demand of the work to empower you to overcome suffering.
(4) **Remain courageous in suffering.** With a willingness to suffer, we must maintain a clear conscience and good behavior and remain fearless in the presence of suffering in the purposeful work of God. (1 Peter 3:14-16)
(5) **Persevere to finish strong.** Consider the work as a race that we must run with endurance, self-control, and discipline to win the crown (1 Corinthians 9:24-26). There will be times when the Lord places demands on a worker and even sleep becomes a luxury so expensive that it must be given away to what is imperative. "…let us run with endurance the race that is set before us, looking unto Jesus, the author and finisher of our faith, who for the joy that was set before Him endured the cross, despising the shame, and has sat down at the right hand of the throne of God" (Hebrews 12:1-2, NKJV).

Have the desire to walk passionately with God. Walking with God is not the same as working for God, although they are related. Walking with God means taking spiritual self-leadership steps to live or abide in the presence of God in all you do, including your work for God. Working for God is completing service for God's purpose by serving others. When Jesus prayed to the Father for strength, it could be considered walking with God. When He died on the cross, it was working for God for His purposeful work of salvation and redemption. It could also, in some sense, mean walking with God. Jesus said, "Abide in me, and I in you" (John 5:4, NIV; Psalms 91:1-3). It means dwelling in the presence of God. Walking with God is a moment-by-moment decision to follow Jesus and His ways to complete the purposeful work or the mission in your life, in the lives of others, and the community. A leader's walk with God involves understanding why he must walk with God, what the mission is, and what the resources are for the daily walk. Then, the leader must walk with consistency, diligence, patience, perseverance, and endurance to accomplish the mission with available resources (Hebrews 12:1-3). The desire to walk with God with passion sustains our work for good works. The leader himself conditions his abilities to sustain his passion for the work, the mind to suffer, and the desire to walk with God. The following examples illustrate this point:

(1) Condition your walk with God. This involves understanding why the leader must walk with God, what the mission is, what the resources are for the daily walk, as well as preparing his mind for whatever the walk requires.

(2) Condition your passion for the work. Cultivate a strong and passionate desire or hunger to understand the purpose of the work.

(3) Condition your mind to suffer to sustain the passion. This involves the ability to finish the work based on the choice you make to have a mind to suffer, which will sustain the passion. No success comes without some sacrifice or suffering.

(4) Condition your mind to triumph over suffering. Great leaders are not frightened by suffering; indeed, they triumph and use the suffering for greater growth.

Understand the Character of God's Workman[12]

The beginning point of developing acts of service is to understand who God's workman is. Paul writes, "For we are His workmanship, created in Christ Jesus for good works, which God prepared beforehand that we should walk in them" (Ephesians 2:10, NJKV).To understand God's plan for work, we must:

Understand that we are the perfect handiwork (art) or skill from God for a specific purpose for God's use. This perfection refers to God's creative plan which He declared to be good and desires for man to serve Him for God's works. Thus, we are not just workers, but we are created to do good works as part of God's preordained plan. Thus, at the core of that purpose is serving God through serving others.

Understand that God's ultimate plan of salvation was to create leaders in Christ Jesus to do good works. God pre-ordained that the worker labors for good works and needs are not ashamed of his work. The ultimate measure of our valid works is the impact the work has on people within the purposeful plan of God.

Understanding the reason for the work was exemplified by Jesus in washing the disciples' feet. It was basically for perfecting the saints, for the spiritual growth of the saints, for edifying the body of Christ and to make others better, "till we all come in the unity of the faith, and of the knowledge of the Son of God, unto a perfect man, unto the measure of the stature of the fullness of Christ" (Ephesian 4:13, NKJV).

Understand the works of the Worker (Leader). As Jesus stated, "He that believeth...the works that do I shall he do also; and greater works than these shall he do also" (John 14:12. NKJV) The work of Jesus is the same as the wo.rk of a leader-servant. Jesus' works included preaching the gospel to the poor, healing diseases and sicknesses, casting out devils, raising the dead, reaching in to meet the needs of others, especially the needy and least among you, and delivering people from tendencies for evil works.

Understand the purpose of the work

How can we understand the purpose of our work for God or our work in the organization in which we serve? The Bible said that before we were conceived, God knew us, and before we were born, he sanctified us for a purpose (Jeremiah 1:5). God predestined a purpose for his children (Romans 8:29). To understand the purpose of the work God has called us to do, we must understand his purpose in our lives. This is also through in your secular lives. You are put in a particular job or employment for a goal to which you must contribute. Martin Luther King Jr. said, "Every person must have a concern for self and feel the responsibility to discover his mission in life. God has given each normal person the capacity to achieve some end. True, some are endowed with more talent than others, but God has left none of us talentless. Potential creative powers are within us, and we have the duty to work assiduously to discover these powers." [16]

Understand the purpose of your life

A leader's important first step in understanding the purpose of his work is to comprehend the reasons for his existence. Rick Warren discussed the following five purposes in The Purpose-Driven Life: You were planned for God's pleasure; you were formed for God's family; you were created to become Christ-like; you were shaped for serving God; you were made for a mission. In his excellent discussions of these five purposes, Dr. Warren said: "If you want to know why you were placed here on this planet; you must begin with God. You were born by His purpose and for His purpose." [15] *Understanding* who we are in God is an important result of understanding God's purpose in our lives. However, the understanding of who we are yields no fruit or action unless we truly grasp the purpose of the work set before us. Until Peter understood the reason for Jesus washing the disciples' feet, he was too proud to follow. The purpose of God's work of salvation is a love of humanity. In training a leader-servant for work, the focus is on training the character, not the skills of the worker 'For it is God who works in you to will and to act according to his good purpose" (Philippians 2:13).

The worker's character must be conditioned for God's excellent purpose. The worker's skills or passion mean nothing to God without a Christ-like character. Remove the character, and the attributes as pillars of Servant leadership, crumble.

SUMMERY 8
DEVELOPING THE ACTS OF SERVANTHOOD-SERVICE

Before starting this exercise, please read and follow the instruction in the preface of this workbook. Answers to these questions are contained in this chapter. Completion of these exercises after reading the chapter should take 60-90 minutes.

Discovering Acts of Servanthood-Service

1. What is servanthood-service?
2. The Servanthood attribute is effective to the extent that the leader has a positive attitude toward the service. What is the role of service attitude other-centered approach in service leadership process?

CHAPTER 8
DEVELOPING THE ACTS OF SERVANTHOOD-SERVICE

3. What are the three primary characteristics of Service in Servanthood ?
4. How can we understand the purpose of our work for God or our work in the organization in which we serve? (Jeremiah 1:5). (Romans 8:29).
5. A leader's important first step in understanding the purpose of his work is to comprehend the reasons for his existence. How can we better *understand* God's purpose in our lives as a way understanding of who we are in God ?(see Philippians 2:13).

Understanding the Principle of Acts of Servanthood-Service

1. People-centeredness is key service in Servanthood. How is a a servant in service said to be people-centered in Servanthood.? What are the appropriate people's skill characteristics a servant must have?
2. The love of humanity is an essential driver for a leader's service that is centered on people. How did God demonstrate this? (John 3:16).
3. In what three ways did Apostle Peter illustrate an example of how we can show the attitude of service by being other's focused (1 Peter 3: 8-13)
4. Passion for service in Servanthood is an essential element for a leader to be conditioned for service leadership. What are three ways passion for the service can be characterized?
5. Read the discussion (ref 1 Corinthians 9:19-27; Hebrews 12:3). What are the six characteristics or results of Paul's passion for service:? What does the passion for work mean?
6. How can passion for work be sustained?
7. What did Apostle Peter mean in his concept of "a mind to suffer" (1 Peter 4:1, NKJV). (1 Peter 2:19-25, NKJV)
8. Or Apostle Paul when he said, "We consistently carry around in our body the death of Jesus, so that the life of Jesus may also be revealed in our body. For we who live are always delivered to death for Jesus' sake, that the life of Jesus also may be manifested in our mortal flesh" (2 Corinthians 4:10-12, NIV).

Practicing the Acts of Servanthood-Service

1. Our work must be evaluated constantly to assess our progress in meeting intended goals. Use the following self-assessment questions to measure your "good" works in service:

Table 8.1: Self-Evaluation of 10-point Tests for service good works		
Rate your bases for service good work (by 1 = never; 2 = almost never; 3 = sometimes; 4= frequently; and 5 =always)		
Tests	Measures/Indicators	Scale 1-5
Faith	Does the work arise out of your active faith and living out the life of Christ in you?	
Glory (Pride)	Does the work bring glory to God or to you?	
Impact.	Does our work impact others—growth and Christ-like fruit that impacts people	
Conformity	Is the work being done in conformity with the written word of God— acts of love and our method of carrying out the work?	
Consistency	Does the work align with a walk with God—consistent walk with God?	
Purpose	Walk with God's purpose for the work of service to others?	
Passion	Walk with passion for the work of service to others?	
Perseverance	Walk with perseverance for the work of service to others?	
Value-added	Does the work add eternal value to the purpose of God for humanity?	
Intentionality	Is the motivation driven by your love and empathy for others	
	Total	____/50

CHAPTER 8
DEVELOPING THE ACTS OF SERVANTHOOD-SERVICE

2. In a sense of purpose of the service, how is a positive sense of purpose in the service an essential element for the service that pleases God and not man?.
3. How did Apostle Paul demonstrate an intentional sense of purpose in service (Galatians 1:10, NKJV)?
4. How can a leader's cultivate humility by a sense of Servanthood (bondservant) toward service?.
5. What did Jesus imply when he said, "Take heed that you do not do your charitable deeds before men, to be seen by them. Otherwise, you have no reward from your Father in heaven" (Matthew 6:1).
6. List the key strategies discussed to cultivate the mind to suffer to sustain the passion for the purposeful work of God (see also 1 Peter 3:14-16; 1 Corinthians 9:24-26; and Hebrews 12:1-2).
7. How can you increase you desire to walk passionately with God.? (John 5:4, NIV; Psalms 91:1-3)
8. The beginning point of developing acts of service is to understand who God's workman is. Paul writes, "For we are His workmanship, created in Christ Jesus for good works, which God prepared beforehand that we should walk in them" (Ephesians 2:10, NJKV). What five things must we understand to fully understand God's plan for His workman in work.

Topic Index

About This Book, 24
Acknowledging
   your imperfections, 71
Acknowledging your weakness, 73
Affective Compassion, 95
authentic, 26, 28, 80, 91
authentic leadership, 39
Authentic Leadership, 47
Authenticity, 45
Boasting
   in Suffering, 75, 91
Characteristics of Leadership
   Servanthood Attribute, 55
Comfort, 43
commitment, 21, 27
Commitment in Sacrifice, 112
Comparisons
   with other works, 42
competence
   in God, 65
Content, 73, 91
credibility, 50
dependence on God, 73
Developing the Acts
   of Servant-Humility, 63, 68
Discipleship
   definition of, 29
distinguishes
   a leader's act of giving, 31
Functional Definitions, 37
Generosity
   definition of, 31
Generosity c, 31
giving, 31
   habit of, 31
humility, 65, 71, 92, 97
   Being authentic, 80, 91
   by depending on God, 81, 91
   developing heart of, 73, 91
Humility, 64, 68
Impact
   of suffering, 77, 90
inside-out, 48

Inspired humility
   by reverence, 98
   by submission, 98
Inspired Humility
   by desire to learn independently, 98
Intelligent Follower, 121
Joshua, 21, 97, 98, 99, 103
law of, 44
Leader as Servant Leadership, 44
   definition, 27
Leader First., 25
Leader-as-Servant Leadership, 25
leaders, 65
leader-servant's affection-attribute
   definition, 50
leadership, 27
Leadership Attributes, 45
Leadership Inner Value system, 27
Mentoring, 97, 103
Model, 25
Moses, 21, 97, 98, 103
Navigation-attribute, 50
Organizational leadership trust, 34
Passion for Good Works, 130
Personal Outward Authenticity, 49
Personal Rights and Privileges, 106, 114
power of God
   in weaknesses, 73, 91
Principle of Servant leadership
   Servanthood Attribute, 56
process, 27
Richness
   of God's power, 73, 91
sacrifice, 105
Selfless Sacrifice, 109
Sense, 127, 134
Servant, 25, 26
service, 105, 130
Stephen Ministry, 61
submission, 98
Submission, 97, 98, 99, 103
Submissive, 97, 103
Teachable Moments to Grow, 100, 103

Teachable Spirit, 83, 92
test
    for leader-servant authenticity, **48**
    of essential elements of personal
        authenticity, **48, 49**
The Leadership Influence-attribute, **43**
Understand
    the Purpose of your life, **132, 133**
walk in God's Presence, **99**
ways of acknowledging
    weakness, **74**
weaknesses, **73, 74**
yoke, **82**

REFERENCES

[1] Greenleaf, R. (1970). *The Servant as Leader,* Indianapolis: The Robert K. Greenleaf Center

[2] Spears, L. (1996). *"Reflections on Robert K. Greenleaf and servant-leadership."* Leadership & Organization Development Journal, 17(7), 33-35

[3] Russell, R.F. (2001). "The role of values in servant leadership." *Leadership & Organization Development Journal,* 22(2), 76-83

[4] Russell, R.F., and Stone, A.G. (2002). "A review of servant leadership attributes: developing a practical model." *Leadership & Organization Development Journal,* 23(3), 145-15

[5] Terry. R. W (1993). *Authentic Leadership: Courage In Action,* San Francisco, CA ,Jossey-Bass

[6] George, B (2003). *Authentic Leadership: Rediscovering the Secrets to Creating Lasting Value.* San Francisco, CA, Jossey-Bass

[7] Shamir, B. & Eilam, G. (2005). "What's your story? Toward a life-story approach to authentic leadership." Leadership Quarterly, 16, 395–418.

[8] Anderson, GL (2009). Advocacy Leadership: Toward a Post-Reform Agenda in Education, Routledge, New York, 41

[9] Yacobi, B.G. *"Elements of Human Authenticity."* http://www.philosophytogo.org /wordpress/?p=1945, Retrieved, July 15, 2012

[10] George, B (2003). *Authentic Leadership: Rediscovering the Secrets to Creating Lasting Value,* San Francisco, CA, Jossey-Bass

[11] Wosu, SN (2014), *Leader as Servant Leadership Model,* Xulon Press

[12] Nee, Watchman (1988). *The Character of God's Workman,* Christian Fellowship Publisher, NY

[13] Slamka, S (2010). "Humility as a Catalyst for Compassion The Humility-Compassion Cycle of Helping Relevance to Counseling." College of St. Joseph In Vermont

http://compassionspace.com/sg_userfiles/revised_humility-compassion.pdf], Retrieved, July 2012

[14]Collins, Jim (2001). *Good to Great: Why Some Companies Make the Leap... and Others Don't* , Harper Business

[15]Warren, R (2002) *The Purpose Driven Life,* Published by Zondervan.

[16]King, Martin L, Jr. *The Strength of Love,* Pocket Books, 1964, p. 69).

[17]Stevenson, Mary. *"Footprints in the Sand."* http://www.footprints-in-the-sand.com/index.php?page=Poem/Poem.php.

[18]Nelson Mandela (1994). *Long walk to Freedom,* Little, Brown and Company, New York

[19]Wosu, SN (2014). *Leader as Servant Leadership Model,* Xulon Press,

www.ingramcontent.com/pod-product-compliance
Lightning Source LLC
LaVergne TN
LVHW061550070526
838199LV00077B/6988